CONVERSATIONS

BRIDE SONGS AND PSALMS TO THE

King

RAELYNN PARKIN

Cover designed by Jamacia Johnson Text

SpiriTruth Publishing Company
Your multi-platform publishing partner
7710-T Cherry Park Drive, Suite 224
Houston, Texas 77095
www.WorldwidePublishingGroup.com
(713) 766-4272

EBook: 978-1-312-97174-5

Paperback: 978-1-312-97172-1

Hardcover: 978-1-312-97173-8

Published in the United States of America.

Table of Contents

Dedication

This book is dedicated to all the worshippers who have longed for deeper realms of worship and more intimate expression!

To my husband who has been Jesus to me and supported me through all the good and bad.

To my children who love to worship with me and to all my family who have supported me through the years.

To all my mentors, teachers, and fellow worshippers who have shared their love of worship and to the amazing prophetic instrumentalists and singers who shared their beautiful gifts with me.

To Eddie and Alice Smith and everyone involved with SpiriTruth Publishing who gave a voice to this expression!

And to my Lord Jesus Christ for His song to me and the Holy Spirit for breathing life into my Song!

Preface

This book represents over 20 years of my life and all of the beautiful love songs that the Lord has sung over me. Many of the poetic expressions are conversations between the Lord and myself and as the Lord stirred my heart to return in my love walk with Him, I believe these psalms and songs will stir others in their return to their first love. As you begin to partake of them, you will begin to see common themes of the Bride and the King, the Authority of the Bride and the Lovesick heart longing for her heart's desire!

Many have asked me over the years about how I worship and how to enter these deeper, more intimate places with the Lord. I believe it has been a gift from the Lord Himself, and He has given me voice to share it with the remnant Bride who has eyes to see and ears to hear what the Spirit of the Lord is saying to this last hour generation of worshippers. But my heart says that the Lord cannot help himself and He is drawn to a purity and a heart that longs for Him! I believe that you cannot kiss Him that He does not Kiss you back! And you know when you have been kissed by Him!

I also believe that the Lord is not returning for less than what He left in the earth, but for the fruition, the fully mature harvest, and the Mature Bride who has prepared herself to be presented to the Holy and Righteous King. She will be a Glorious and Righteous Bride deserving of the King of Kings Himself! Many have asked over the years when do you think He is coming? The Lord spoke to my Heart, "Watch the Bride! For she is a mere reflection of the King and the closer He is to her the more Glorious she shall become! Watch the Bride!

7

I encourage you to savor these words as most have been mere dictation and spoken from His mouth to my heart! Allow them to sweep you away in Holy Preparation for A Personal encounter and visitation from the King Himself! And visit them often, and allow your heart to be awakened to the Passionate Longing of Your King for You! Make them your own and share them with the Remnant Bride who is longing for more…The Kiss…The Embrace… The Dance…

Come away with me…

Raelynn Parkin

BRIDE PSALMS
POETRY
of the
Heart

Hidden Treasures

Uncover the hidden treasures
Discover the hidden pearls of wisdom
Open up the things that lie dormant
Bring forth the untapped springs of living water

Remove the things that hinder you
Those things that cover up your life
That long to spring forth
Uncap the hidden wells, the fountains of life.

Let joy come forth in the birth of new things.
Let joy come forth in new beginnings
Let the fire return of lost hopes and dreams
Let the Heavenly Winds come that bring the change

That cause me to soar in heights I have not known
On wings of destiny,
Your Breath leading me
Your Kiss enveloping me
Your gentle whisper guiding me.

To move beyond the things I've known
To follow you through deeper waters
I long to be immersed in the deepest waters of your love
For your love is leading me to the Place of Your Glory
To the place of Your Destiny
To the place where purpose is ignited
To go beyond the things I've strived for
To know only the Voice who loves me
To the place of divine security

To the knowing of who I am in you

To understand who you've called me to be
To manifest Your Glory
To manifest Your Presence
To see your eyes of fire in mine
To feel your fire burn inside of me.

I want to know you.
I want to feel you.
I want to see you.
I want to hear you.
I want to love you, to worship you, to woo you as a lover.

To drink you in to discover
Just who this King of Glory is.
To be swept away in your embrace
To be impassioned by your kiss
To be set on fire as your eyes look through me

To see the things you put in me
To activate my destiny
To call me forth in purpose
To call me by my name.

For you have called me for such a time as this
You've hidden me for my reserved purpose.
You have not set me aside
You have not forgotten me

But you have hidden me in the cleft of the Rock
You did not forget where you left me.

I hear you now summon me forth
To come out of the hidden place
I feel your hand bring me forth
And it is not just a level place
You are bringing me to a higher place

A place of promotion, A place of elevation,
A place where others will see the hidden things
You formed in me.

For as I was hidden for a time
When your crowning and coronation come forth
I shall remain hidden in you.
That all they see in me is You
The King of Glory crowned in splendor.

For I am seated with you in heavenly places
My eyes are fixed upon Your face
I long to stay in your heavenly embrace
I long for your kiss upon my life.

For you are all I see, all that I know,
All that I long to be.
I long for you to be manifest in me.
The fullness, Your stature, Your Glory.
I don't want to just know part
I want to know your fullness
I want to live continually in your Presence.
That your Presence envelopes me, surrounds me,
Affixes me to the Rock.
That as you are, so am I in the earth.

In the Fullness, in the Measure, in the Stature of Christ
In the Fullness, in the Measure, in the Stature of Christ
In the Fullness, in the Measure, in the Stature of Christ

Come Lord Jesus come
Come Lord Jesus come
Come Lord Jesus come, Come.

Let your Bride walk where you walked.
Let your Bride rise higher to the place you've called her.
That she will walk by your side
As your fire burns within her.
That your Holy Desire ignites her
That your passion consumes her in your Love.

That your eyes of love call her
To rise above her ashes
To dance upon the places that used to bind her
To find her place of destiny
To stand in her place of purpose
To release the hidden dreams you locked away
For this time and this place
Open up the doors of her heart.
Unlock the dreams of her life (heart)

Open the treasures within
Bring forth the destiny within.

Open her eyes that she may see her hidden beauty
Release her from the former things
That bound her and held her down
Unlock her purpose within

Open her trust again.

Make all things new again
Let her dance like a child again
Let her sing the songs of her youth
Let her feel the safety of your Hand
As you lift her up from the depths
To a higher place you've called her to walk in.

Out of the dry places
Onto the River banks
To go into the deeper waters
Where she feels your presence surround her
A place of total dependence
Upon your Spirit to guide her

You're calling her to the deeper things
You're calling her to come up higher
To come up from the low lands
To come up from her valley
To come up to the mountain
Where your Glory dwells
Come up into the Cloud that looks like a consuming fire.
Come and find your rest
Come and find your residence in my Presence
Come where few have ventured
Come and sit where I am.
I've waited for you forever to come and be with me
That where I am there you may be also.

Come and sit with me awhile
Come and find your rest

Come enjoy my Presence
Drink of my love for you

Be refreshed in Living Waters
Let me fill you to overflowing
Let me satisfy you in ways you've never known
Let me bring you into my Holy Desire

For my fire of purpose shall ignite you
My flame in you shall show brighter
It will be a fire you can't contain
An all consuming fire.

Offer up yourself as a living sacrifice
Come to my altar and offer yourself
My fire shall not destroy you
But my fire shall refine you
It shall cause the dross to come off of you
Shall remove the impurities from you
The things you could not change
Those things you could not do for yourself
Shall lift off of you
Shall separate and be removed from you
In my fire, my all consuming fire
You shall come out of my fire
Changed, rearranged
Into the one I've called you to be.
The one who looks like my Son
The one who manifests my Glory
One who radiates my Splendor
One who exudes the beauty of my Holiness
One without blemish, without spot or wrinkle

The Manifested Bride of the Holy King
The Glorious Bride radiating His Fire to the world.
That draws them to the light of His Beauty
That causes all men to see

The Living Sacrifice that has become
Holy, Holy to the Lord
Holy, Holy to the Lord,
Holy, Holy to the Lord, Holy.

For you are set apart
You are consumed in His Fire
You are destined to stand beside Him
As He comes forth in His Glory.

The Holy King and His Royal Bride
Standing side by side
For all the world to witness
The Marriage Supper of the Lamb
His royal seal set upon her
His signet ring upon her finger
Crowned with His Royal Purpose
Adorned in His royal Garments
He has extended His Scepter
For her to accept and to uphold
To declare and decree
With his Power and Authority
She is crowned as Esther
She shall have the ability
To remove the head of the enemy
That dared to destroy his People

She shall stand tall in her purpose
For she was set aside and called to this purpose.
For the Lord says, "I called her forth in her mother's womb
And her destiny I called forth in the earth.
She shall raise up a people
She shall ignite destiny
With the Flame of Ignited Desire that flows from Her King.
She shall call them forth to take their stand
Calling a mighty army in the Land
With Holy Armor that shall withstand the darts of the
enemy.
Rise up, rise up, rise up
To the Place I've called you
Rise up, rise up, rise up
To the Place I've called you
Rise up, rise up, rise up
To the Place I've called you.

My Presence shall surround you
The enemy shall not inhibit you
My Purpose for you shall ignite you
I'm calling you with my loving whisper
I'm changing you into my Stature
I'm filling you with my Glory
That you shall know me as I know you
You shall hear my voice, even my whisper

Above the clanging noises of this world
You shall feel my spirit
As he draws you to my secret place.
Where you will come often
So I may fill you up.

For you hear my Voice singing over you.
I have awakened you to hear my song.
I have been singing over you all night long.
For I love you, and you feel my love for you
For I have longed to come to this place
Where I am with you.
Come away for awhile
Let my love cover you..."

Let us Ascend

Let us ascend to your Holy Mountain
Where your Glory dwells
Let us go up into the Cloud of your Glory
Let your Presence surround us, fill us, warm us.
Let the weight of your Glory cover us.
Let your atmosphere of Heaven envelope us

Descend upon us with liquid drops of Glory
Let it be a place where Heaven dwells
A hidden place of rest for your people
A place of revelation where we
Come to know just who you are
And who we are in you
A holy place where we are
Changed, where we exchange
Our weakness for your strength
Our sorrow for your joy
Our weary souls for your rest
Our brokenness for wholeness

We've come to sit with you awhile
To partake of the flesh that is your Word
To drink of the new wine in your Blood
To look upon the One who loves us,
Who comforts us.
We long to drink of the Pleasure
Of the River of Heaven
For there is joy in Your Presence
We long to know the security and the safety
Of our Shepherd's Hand

We have come to drink of your cup
That you would fill us up
That your joy would overflow
And we would come to know
Your love for us, in us, thru us.

We've come to drink of the cup of your Holy Desire
We've come that you would consume us in your Holy Fire
Your righteous fire that purifies us
We've come to a place where we could not go
Unless you lead us here by your Spirit

A valley of decision, a place of circumcision
A place of consecration, a place of visitation.
A place of revelation where your love covers us
Changes us into the Image of the I AM.
The gentle quiet Lamb of rest
The Roaring Lion of Praise
That goes before his mighty army.

You are assembling a mighty host of hidden ones
That are coming to the forefront
That shall confront the enemy
As mighty weapons in your Hand.
They shall not fear but stand up tall
For through it all
You've prepared them in your fire.

The enemy cannot defeat this mighty host
You've raised up by your Hand
They shall not be overcome, undone or overrun
For you have raised them in the land.

They shall run to the battle lines
With a shout of Victory
Faith goes before them.
Your Glory surrounds them
In unity they shall withstand
Their light shall dispel darkness
And push back the hand of the enemy.
The Boldness of the Sword shall come forth

For they cannot be contained.
They are sustained by the Love of their God.
For they know the times and the seasons
They know the time they've been called to
They will not shrink back in fear
For they know the Voice of their Captain
The Command of the Lord of Hosts

Their peace is their weapon
The Love of God securely holds them in place
They are trained in the strategies
Exercised with their weaponry
Empowered with His Authority
Emboldened by the Courage of their Christ.

They shall arise in Victory
Awakened from their slumber
Greater in number than you have ever seen.
For these hidden ones have come out of their caves
They shall come out in waves of His Glory
They've been refined through his Fire
Empowered this hour to do
Great damage to the enemy

For He has been their Rock, their Resurrection

He is raising them up from the heap of their ashes
He is calling them to Holy Purpose
The abandoned ones, the forgotten ones,
The betrayed ones, the stranded ones
He has remembered them and not forgotten their cries.
He is bringing them out for the world to see
With great Power and Authority

They shall receive the recompense of the Lord by His Hand
They have been bought for the price of His Salvation
They shall not be moved from their course
They are a great force to be reckoned with

They are the Army of his Mighty Ones
The Generals in the Land
The Deborahs, the Esthers,
Moses and Elijah
Glory and Fire are coming forth
The Strength of Heaven
The Angelic Hosts are with them.

Breakthrough is coming
Breakthrough is piercing the darkness
Light of His Glory is going forth, its penetrating.
The Heavens are opened up
The Voice of the Father is heard in the land.

These are my Beloved Sons and Daughters
In whom I am well pleased
They are standing in the Image of My Son

They are One with me, with my will, with my Purpose.

The Holy Spirit is descending upon them
Covering them with His Mighty Wings.
Shielding them in His Great Peace.
Igniting them with the Holy Fire of Heaven's Flame
The Winds of His Spirit have begun to blow in the land.

Winds of Heaven's Change are swirling around them.
They are empowered as agents of change
To rearrange the unseen plans of the enemy.
They are stealth warriors sent to uncover strategies
Discover plans of the enemy

To bring them to naught
To wield the Sword of Destruction
To the enemy of His Purpose
To bring down strongholds
To expose lofty imaginations
To shout down walls of religion
To liberate a captive people
To the freedom of Christ.

Pharoah and Babylon shall not withstand
Holy commands of the One True Living God.
They have come to liberate the Remnant Church
That they shall worship the Holy King
There shall be a dividing line
For those who come out and those who stay
So hear the Word of Moses
"Let my people go.
Let my people go.

Let my people go."

Come out of your captivity
Come out into your liberty
Come out of the bondage that has enslaved you
The system of religion that has deceived you.
The Word of Christ calls you out.
He has called you out of religion
Into relation, communion with Him.
He has called you out of your hard labor
Into the resting place with Him.

Where you shall rest upon the Breast of Christ
You shall hear his heartbeat
And feel the warmth of His Breath
His Love shall settle you
His Grace shall overwhelm you
His Glory shall satisfy you
His Spirit shall overcome you.
The hurried life, the busy life shall be silenced
For his peace has come to bring you new life
The Prince of Peace shall dwell in your heart.
You shall know the height, the depth, the length, the breadth
Of the Love of Christ
You shall be unmoved in the Love of Christ.

Nothing can separate you from the Love of Christ
Feel His Love spread over you
Feel His Love cover you
Feel His Love wash over you
Feel His Love that satisfies you…

The Hidden Ones

Let Your Healing rivers flow
Living waters that wash over us
The Balm of Gilead that heals, restores,
Comforts, soothes, renews.
You're calling us out of desolation
Isolation, separation.
Out of our dying places,
Out of trials and tribulations
For we did not love our lives so much
That we could not lay them down.
For there was a price that was to be paid
A price for your Glory to come
You are calling us forth out of our ashes
Out from the fires of refinement
Out from the fire upon your altar

It did not please you to hear our crying
It pleased you that in our dying
The Image of your Son was forged
In your Heavenly Fires

The Fragrance of Worship has begun
From your fiery altar
The Incense of Prayer has won.
And has gone before the path you paved
For your Promises to come forth

For God has not forgotten his dying ones.
The ones who paved the path for life to come

It's time to throw off former things
That held us, that bound us,
The grave clothes of yesterday
You're calling us to a new and living way
Days you have ordained of destiny
Days of purpose, days of promises
Written down words of remembrance
Words of intercession for things you're going to do.

Holy is the purpose of his Mighty Ones,
His Hidden ones, his Dying ones,
Their lives under his altar, crying,
"When shall all these things be,
And when shall we see the recompense of the Lord,
The vengeance of our King?"

These living, dying ones shall see
The Hand of the Lord bring them forth
They shall go through his hidden doors
That their dying paid for
The Glory cost them everything
A new song shall He bring
From their hidden place in Him
A New Song shall rise in the Land
Orchestrated by His Hand
Accompanied by Heaven
Angels shall ascend and descend
Above the place of resurrection.

The sounds of Heaven shall be heard in the earth
The harmonies of saints and angels
Shall proclaim the Coming of the Risen King

Melodies of Heaven's Glory
Shall accompany the Bride's adorning
As she is prepared to be presented to Her King.

The Oils of His Spirit have saturated her
The Beauty of the Lord has adorned her countenance
She is clothed in Righteous Robes of Splendor
And crowned in majestic favor
Her days of anonymity are gone
She shall be presented before the world
And all shall know there is a Queen in the land.
She shall petition her king on behalf of her people
She shall proclaim liberty in the land
Deliverance from their captivity
The Land of the Living shall it be again.

This is a day of resurrection
From former insurrection
A day of Holy Unity, a Holy Community
A remnant Bride rising from her ashes
A jubilant Church taking her stand.
A shout of Victory heard again in the land.

A mighty army marching in line
In sync, in purpose with their King
His Mighty Sword dividing
His true ones from the sleeping.

A time to choose, a time to obey
The Word of the Lord this day
He's calling you to his new way
The Higher path paved in his Peace.

Do not be conformed to this world
But be transformed in your renewed mind
Come out of the patterns of the world.
Come into the Holiness of the Lord.
Set your mind on things that are above
Things that are inhabited with His Love

For His love will fill you and satisfy you
Replace your lack and your need
And you will know joy unspeakable
For His Glory shall overwhelm you
His Peace shall surround you
His Purpose shall raise you
His Authority shall empower you
His Favor shall go before you
And you will know your King.

Fear shall not overcome you
For he has emboldened you with Faith
And you shall know His Voice
You will hear his heartbeat in your ear
Your heart is made complete in Him
For He has come to capture you with His Presence
His Loving Gaze has steadied you
His embrace has guided you
His Kiss has ignited you
And you are His Beloved
You are His Beloved.

You are His Treasure
You are His Cherished Ones
You are His Inheritance

You are His Royal Priesthood
You are His Holy Nation

Those the world has forgotten, abandoned
Those are His Chosen Ones
The foolish ones that confound worldly wisdom
Their faces are set like flint
Unmoved and unshaken
In the face of worldly destruction
They are empowered to take possession of their
Promised Land.
They are crossing over from familiar shores
Comfort zones that no longer fit them.

Their feet walk swiftly on dry ground
Though walls of water surround them
The Spirit of Promise is guiding them
In ways they have not known
In places they have not gone before
They shall know which way to go
In higher realms of His Spirit
In higher dimensions with Him

His Word is coming alive in them
Paving their path with illumination
Igniting their steps with Purpose
Leading to Days of Destiny

These are the jealous ones
For His Holiness and Purity
These are the desperate Ones
For the revelation of His Glory

His Holy Desire has consumed them
His Spirit has set them on fire
They are engulfed in Flames of Revival
They spark His Bride with embers of renewal
They shall set this world on fire
Then He shall bring rains of cleansing
Rains of renewal
Rains of Washing…

The King's Procession

Lord you've taken my hand
You have led me to the dance
I feel the power of your embrace
Surrounded by your Glory and grace
I hear you whisper my name
I hear you call me by name
You call me lovely
And that I am worthy of this place with you.
I'm swept away by Your Desire
You're calling me to come higher
To walk in paths of destiny
You have laid out before me
I feel the ease within Your Grace
In the former place of striving and contending
For your kingdom's sake

You are driving out enemies of former days before me
Your Presence goes before me
Your Presence amazes me
As your Glory surrounds me
And your spirit calls within me
Come higher to the place I've prepared for you.
Steal away with My Presence
As my Word awakens you
My Revelation ignites you
My Wisdom and Knowledge call you
To the place of my discernment.
In the place of my Power where Purity reigns
In Heaven's Flame that births my Kingdom in the earth.
And causes all things to align with My Word

That clears out the atmosphere
And prepares for the appearing of the Lord.
The Coming of Heaven's King
Accompanied by his Heavenly Host
And Clouds of witnesses cheering
The Approaching King of Glory
The King's Procession has come into view
As the King enters His Sanctuary
His Dwelling among His People
His Tabernacle of Glory residing
A Habitation of Heaven
Surrounding His Holy Remnant
His Faithful ones forged in His Holy Fire
Mighty Weapons in His Hand
Meant for the destruction of the enemy's plans.
Front Line Warriors scarred in battle
With Clanging Swords and shields that rattle
The enemy's camp.
For confusion has descended upon them
As Heaven's perception has brought clarity of vision.
Clearly defined purpose
Unabashed Confidence
In the One who is leading them
By His Loving Word
And His Trumpet Call
Unflinched in their resolve
To follow Him in his battle call.
To dispel darkness with His Heavenly Light
That shines in their countenance
And reflects in their eyes of fire
That is fixed upon His Gaze.
They have come out from their wilderness days

And their famine filled ways
To discover springs of Living Water
Flowing upon dry desert lands.
Refreshed by Waters from His Hand

They shall arise from their poverty
Their poor spirit hungering for the Presence of their God
Thirsting for the Righteousness of His Kingdom
Filled and satisfied in their Purpose
He is calling forth this new generation
That will boldly proclaim the Holy Nation
His Royal Priesthood that exudes His Holiness
And walks before Him in Uprightness
They are clothed in His Righteousness
Prepared in His Secret Place

They shall release the sounds of Heaven
The sounds that bring Heaven to earth
Sounds united with Angelic voice
Accompanied with Heaven's orchestration
The sound that calls the Assembly
To come to the mountain of Glory
The sound of trumpets that
Bring down walls of separation
That tear down walls of division

Sounds that release Heaven's war commands
Strategies of Victory for the Land
Sounds that restore faith in the earth
The Sounding cry of New Birth
The cry of the Man child in the earth.
The Isaac of Promise to be delivered

Written Promises He has remembered
His Faithfulness shall be heralded
His Might and Goodness shall be exalted
All nations shall bow before him
His Glory shall precede Him
As His Majesty and Splendor surround Him.
For He is worthy to be praised
The Lion of Judah is Holy
And he shall rule and reign with Grace
His Glory shall fill the earth

Let us release the sounds of Heaven
Let us release the voice of the Lord
Let us release his sound of many waters
Let us release his sound in the earth.

For He inhabits the praise of his people
He inhabits the sounds of Heaven
He inhabits the release of his voice in Heaven
He inhabits the release of His Sound in the earth.

For in Heaven the angels sing
Holy, Holy, Holy is the Lord God Almighty
Who was and is and is to come.
And as His Holiness is declared
The One True Living God
Demonstrates His Glory.

And His Glory fills all of Heaven
His Glory inhabits Heaven
Heaven is a habitation of His Glory
Heaven resounds His Glory

His Glory inhabits Heaven's sound
And at the declaration of His Holiness
Demonstration of His Glory comes.

The Elders lay prostrate before Him
With crowns in hand lifted up
Crying, "Worthy is the lamb
Worthy is the Lamb who was slain for us
Worthy is the Lamb
Worthy is the Lamb who died for us
Worthy is the Lamb."

And the angels join the elders
As the sounds of Heaven agree
Heaven resounds with His Glory
Heaven resounds with Harmony
As angels and elders agree,
"Holy is the Lord
Worthy is the Lamb."

And the Four Living Creatures
Move and have their being
Wheel within wheel
Moving in four directions
Moving with Resounding Glory
Moving with the Glory,
Here and there, wheel within wheel.
Moving in all directions
Moving as the Glory moves
Moving and being
Resounding, agreeing
Sounds of Heaven agreeing while

Angels and elders are declaring
Holy is the Lord
Worthy is the Lamb.

As elders and angels agree in Heaven
All citizens of Heaven are immersed in Glory
In harmony, in melody.
He inhabits the sounds of the Praise of Heaven
Heaven is a habitation of His Glory
His Glory resounds in Heaven
Chorus of Heaven agreeing
Releasing the Sounds of Heaven
His Glory resonates in the sounds of Heaven Releasing

On earth as it is in Heaven
The Sounds of Inhabited People
Sounds of the Remnant Church
Sounds of the Glorious Church
Resounding and releasing
Sounds of agreement with Heaven

The Glorious Church releasing the sound
That angels harmonize in agreement
A Habitation of Glory
A Habitation of Heaven
Invading with agreement
With the Inhabiting Praise of His People
The Lord inhabits the Sound of his people.
The Lord inhabits the release of His Voice

The Lord inhabits the Sound of many waters
Inhabiting the Sounds released in the earth through his
Bride.

The Bride is releasing her agreement of Heaven
The Bride resounds the Inhabiting sounds
The Lord inhabits the sound of His Voice
Released in His Church
Agreeing with citizens of Heaven
A Habitation of Glory is coming to the earth
A dwelling of Glory invading the earth
Through release of his sound of Heaven
Thru release of the Bride's Revelation
Thru resounding of instruments orchestrating
The Demonstration of His Glory
The manifest Presence of the Lord
An Invasion of Glory manifesting in His Church in the earth
Resembles and radiates the Sound of Heaven.
A Habitation of Glory

Thy Kingdom come, thy will be done
On earth as it is in Heaven
Blessing and honor, Glory and Power
On earth as it is in Heaven

Glory radiating, Glory manifesting
Breakout of Glory
Breakout of Revelation
Breakout of the Sounds of Heaven
Breakout of Inhabiting Praise
Breakout of the Sounds of many waters
Breakout of Glory that waters the earth.

Breakout of the Hovering Spirit of God
That broods upon the waters of the deep, deep, deep
Springing forth from his people

Holy Spirit brood again upon the deep waters of your
people
Brooding on the waters of your Spirit People
Brooding upon the release of your people
Brooding upon the release of the sound of
Your Remnant Church

Releasing the Voice of the Lord
Releasing the Sound of many waters
Holy Spirit brood upon the sound of many waters
The Sound of the voice of the Lord
Being released from the Glorious Church

That your glory may cover the earth again
As Your waters cover the sea
Let your waters brood over the earth
Released as sounds of many waters that cover the sea.
Your Glory inhabiting the sounds of many waters

Releasing the sounds of Heaven
Releasing the Glory of the Bride
A Sound that radiates your Glory
A Sound that is inhabited of the Lord
The Sound of the Voice of the Lord
Inhabited by His Glory in His Bride.

We are His Habitation
We are His Glory
We release the sounds of Heaven
We release agreement in the earth
We say yes to the sounds of Heaven
We agree with the sound of Heaven
We are his Heaven on earth
We release His Glory through our sound
His Glory manifests in our sound
As His Glory inhabits Heaven
His Glory inhabits his Voice
The Sound of Many waters
Released in the earth

The Sound of many waters released in his Bride
His Bride carries the Voice of his Love
His Bride carries the Glory of the King
As his Bride releases the Sound of his Glory
His Bride releases His Glory in the earth.
On earth as it is in Heaven
His Glory fills all of Heaven
Heaven's Glory is released in the earth.

The sounds of earth align in one chorus
With the sounds of Heaven
Then all agree that He is holy
Heaven and earth sing He is Holy
Heaven and earth agree He is worthy
Heaven and earth are filled with his Glory
Endless streams of Glory
Flowing between Heaven and earth

As the Crystal Sea flows before the Throne
Rivers of His Love flow from Heaven to the earth

Rivers of Life agree in His Glory
As we release the sounds of Heaven
As we release His Glory in the earth
As we release the voice of many waters
We release the life of his rivers
Flowing in us thru us from Heaven

We release the life of his river in the earth
Thru the sounds of Heaven we hear
The sounds of Heaven resound in the earth
The waters flowing that release life to the earth

As the waters of His Life come to the earth
The waters refresh and bring His Life
To dry parched ground of humanity
That needs the waters that bring His Life.

We shift the sounds of earth
We shift to sounds of Heaven
That Heaven and his True Church agree that He is Holy
That earth is filled with glory
As waters that cover the sea…

The Glorious Bride

My Glory is your treasure
There is Glory in my Presence
When you come to sit in my Glory
You will know the depths of My Presence

I am shaking the earth again
The world's not shaking on its own
I am shaking, I am sifting
My Remnant church I am sifting out.

Those things that can be shaken
Shall fall off of her
Her sacrifice shall she offer me
That she will be adorned in My Radiance
My Glory shall rest upon her countenance.

Let no fear take residence with you
For the shakings are by My Hand
And you have known my Hand in yours
Trust that my hand shall preserve you.

I am calling out my remnant heart
My heart that resides in my Bride
These are days of Destiny I'm leading you to.
For my Glory shall rest upon you.

I am preparing you as a Glorious Bride
One without blemish, spot, or wrinkle.
Once my fires have forged you in the secret place
My refining fire shall reveal the I AM.

For I formed you in the image of the Son
My fires shall release the Glorious One.
The Fires of my altar shall reveal My Son
The Lion of Judah, Victorious One.

For there was a day when you said, "Yes, Lord."
You came to my altar as a living sacrifice
Your willingness to die has chosen you
You did not shrink back your cries.
But you embraced my Love in the dying times.

You trusted my heart when nothing made sense
You remembered me in the depths of the heat
I have remembered the price you paid.

There is a price for the Weight of my Glory
Many are not willing to pay
Your Love for me compelled you further
My Love for you shall raise you higher.

I've called an end to your wilderness
Your wilderness has served its purpose
The things forged in the fire shall reveal the warrior
My Fires shall reveal the Holy One.

I shall astonish the world through you.
They will wonder where you came from
I have taught you to stay hidden in my Presence
From your hidden place I shall be revealed.

What was left of you was burned in my fire
Your dying remains before me night and day

I have not forgotten you, nor forsaken you.
Your cries in the night have come before me
They were not just personal inconvenience,
But they were cries of intercession
The Incense of your prayers have come before me
For you longed for my Glory to be revealed.

Know that the days before you are greater
The Glory of yesterday has not been lost
For my Fire produced a greater Glory
A higher place that I have brought you to.

I have called you to run ahead of my army
I called you to pave a path with your life
That others may run on this forged path
My army shall be raised up quickly.

I have called you as a general of this mighty Army
I have written my commands upon your life
You know my Hand and you hear my Voice
That leads you in the way to go.

No longer will they just hear your voice
They will hear my voice above yours
I have set my seal upon your life
I have crowned you in My Authority

Your obedience to me has made you dangerous
For when you hear my Voice you're quick to follow
All hesitation has ceased its calling
My command has emboldened you.
My Fiery love has impassioned you

In this place that I have brought you to
Fear has been silenced, it has no pull on you.

My Mighty Army shall arise in the Land
They shall be in sync with my Heart and my Purpose.
The world shall know what I have resurrected
I am raising up my Church again.

No longer shall she remain silent
The voice of the Roaring Lion shall resound in her
When the Lion of Judah's voice is released in her
The darkness shall bow its knee to me
The darkness shall part like the Red Sea
And it shall make way for the Light to come

The voices of darkness shall say, Yes Lord
They shall be silenced at the Appearing of My Bride
Radiant in my Glory
Manifesting my Power
Raised up to reclaim the lands I promised
Revealing the Resurrected One
Decreeing by My Authority that I died to give her.

All authority has been given to me
In demonstration of my Love for her
All authority has been given to her

For I guard over My Words in her mouth
That is where I placed My Sword
It is mighty to conquer armies
It shall silence all her enemies.

Then all will know that I have spoken
My Presence accompanies my Voice
I move Heaven and earth to do what I have spoken
It brings me joy to see My Image arise in her.

So arise my church arise.
Yesterday is gone, its over
This is a new Day that I have called you to
A highway of Holiness I'm bringing you to.

The days of low living are over
You are called to soar upon the heights with me.
Keep your eyes fixed upon my gaze
Those things that move others shall not touch you.

Follow in the ways of my Holiness
Give place only to the things I've told you
You shall not crawl or walk as you did before
For now it's time to run.

You shall run ahead and know the plans of the enemy
Keenly aware of the strategies he's planned
No longer shall he triumph over you,
For he is exposed and he is undone.

No longer shall he sabotage My Plan for you
For I have called you to be a great Saboteur
With my Word shall the enemy be undone
The battles of yesterday are gone.

For I am the Victor and I have won
Battles that took years shall be won in a day

Those battles strengthened you for war
Though you bear the scars of former skirmishes
Those scars shall bring forth My Honor.

For I chose to display my scars for all eternity
They speak of My greatest Victory
I wear them because of my Love for you
That you will know that I've already won.

So go forth in my Confidence
Know that I am always with you
The Victorious One is at your side
The Holy King and His Radiant Bride

For you are consumed in my Holy Fire
All they see is Me in you
You in me and I in you
There is no separation.

My love shall sustain you
My Word shall preserve you
My faith shall embolden you
My Authority shall arise in you
My Glory shall be revealed in you.

Do not marvel at what is coming out of you
For it is I the Holy One revealed in you...
Now rest in this...

A King of Their Choosing

They asked for a King of their choosing
One who is head and shoulders above the rest
My Faithful have asked for the King of Glory
To be enthroned once again in the land.

That I may sit in my seat of honor
That true justice shall come from my Hand
The enemy has launched an all out offense
His arsenal has been revealed.

But I have not finished what I started.
My people shall rejoice in My Victory
For I won before I ever started
My Victory was sure before the foundations.

When I speak the Final Word it shall be done
You will declare the King is Worthy
The King is Holy
The Mighty Victorious One
The King of Glory.

I shall reveal you in my purpose
You shall sit beside me on my Throne
You are seated with me in Heavenly places
All of Heaven rejoices in what I've done.

Take heart as you are watching the unfolding
For I have overcome the world
Though she rages and accuses you
My victory shall come to you quickly

So rest in what I have given you
Let my Peace wash over you
Let my Glory reside upon you
Let my Love uphold you
Let my Joy strengthen you

Rest in my Secret Place
Rest in the Hidden place
Days of anonymity are coming to an end
My Glory shall I reveal in you…

Adorned

Soaking in the oils of Your Spirit
Bathed in waters of Your Presence
Basking in the Light of Your Glory
Radiating the warmth of your Love

Healed with the Touch of Your Hand
Refreshed by the streams of Your Pleasure
Renewed in the Joy of Salvation
Restored to rise up again

Dressed in garments of Your Favor
Adorned with Pearls of Your Grace
Clothed in arrays of Your Splendor
Crowned as sons of Royalty

The Bride Arising

I'm wooing you as a lover
I long for your embrace
I long for your kiss of worship
Intimate moments with you

I'll take you to the deep
The deep places of My Heart
There I'll teach you to swim
Have no fear, I won't let go.

Places you have never been
Places you can't ever go
Without me leading you there.
I call out to My Beloved
Will you come out and play?
Will you come learn of me
And partake of what I've freely given?

I will adorn you as a Bride
With jewels and Pearls of honor
I will lavish you as My Queen
With treasures untold.
Be still and let me dress you
In My Royal Robes of Righteousness.

Then you may come to me
And ask of me anything
And I'll give it to you.
Ask me anything and I'll give it to you.
The destruction of your enemy

His head on a silver platter,
Up to half of the Kingdom

You have pleased me.
Ask of me, it is yours.
Ask of me, I am yours.

For all these things you already have in me.
All these things I am to you.
Ask and it shall be given unto you.
For as you have humbled yourself as My Bride and My
Queen
My grace in great measure is coming to you.
Grace that gives you strength
Grace that is my Power.
For you shall stand in places you have never known.
My Grace is there for you.
It is your sufficiency.
Let go of who you think you are.
Hold on to who you are in me.
For that is your place of strength, it's hidden in me.

As you rest in the depths of my Heart,
I have arisen as Your Champion.
I am mighty on your behalf to save you.
As you stay in that place of rest in me,
No fear can touch you there.

For I'm your First Husband, and I will give you rest.
I will fight your battles, only rest in me.
I will extinguish your enemies, only rest in me.

I am your Pillar of Cloud by day,
To guide you through the wilderness,
To shield and protect you
From the scorching sun of your trials.
Find joy in me, for I am covering you.

I am your pillar of fire that stands between your enemy and
you.
He cannot even see you through me.

I am taking you across mighty waters
But I am taking you on dry land.
Your foot shall not slip or even get wet.
For I am taking you to the Promise.
The Promise I have made you
You will not see that enemy anymore
For I have destroyed him before your eyes.

Do not forget where I have taken you.
For you need to remember for the battles ahead.
But I have not called you to fight them on your own.
Behold the Mighty Arm of the Lord that goes before you.

My armies of angels are discharged to fight on your behalf.
As you walk in faith, they are in step with you.
If you hold back, and do not go forward,
They will stop and wait for you.

You are my generals and they are awaiting my commands.
I am sending my commands through your mouthpiece.
According to My Authority in you,
For we are marching towards the greatest battle

My church has ever known.
Take heart, I have overcome the world
And I shall overcome the world through you.
Every place your foot touches
Shall be possession of the land taken back in my name.

The enemy may appear to be giants,
But they are quaking in fear
FOR THEY HAVE NEVER SEEN THE BRIDEGROOM
ARISE WITH SUCH POWER IN THE BRIDE AS SHE STEPS
FORWARD.
LOOK, it is HE arising in you
That makes them quake in their boots.
For He is stepping on the property through His Beloved
The enemy is running and leaving all the loot behind.
The Manifested Bride shall take back what the enemy has
stolen from the people of God.
And she leaves a wake of destruction in her path.
All power and authority shall be reestablished to her,
Who represents the Bridegroom, the King.

And He shall come back to receive her unto Himself,
The Glorious Bride adorned as a Queen.
Walking in the full glory of her King.
For as He was in the world, so shall she be.

She has cleaned her garments
And made them spotless and without wrinkle.
Her face radiates the glory of her King
And becomes brighter as He approaches.
She is walking in the power and authority that He left with
her.

She is holy unto Him.
She is wholly His, set apart for only His Touch.

She is more magnificent and more beautiful than He ever
imagined.
The King is enthralled with her beauty.
His breath catches in His Throat as He approaches her.
His love beats passionately in His Heart for her.

And her heart can think of nothing else but the
consummation of His Love,
And the completion of her desire for Him.

The Holy Spirit takes her by the hand
And He delivers her into the hand of her King
As they approach the Wedding Supper of the Lamb.

Written by the Holy Spirit of Promise

Arise O Daughter

Arise, Arise O Daughter of Zion
Arise, Arise Put away your ashen garments
Arise, Arise Put on my Garments of Splendor
I've called you to wear my garments of Glory
I've adorned you in garments of strength
Put on, put on my garments of Glory
Put on my garments of Power
Put on my garments of authority
Arise I'm calling you to a dance
I'm calling you to dance above the circumstance
I'm calling you to come higher
The circumstance can't touch you here

Arise and take up your position
Arise and take your place by my side
I've adorned you as a queen as my bride
Come take your stand, we're going for a ride.
Arise my Church my Bride
Arise My Church My Bride
Arise My Beloved
Take my hand you're gonna stand with me
Arise shake off yesterday
Arise shake off the circumstance
Arise and shake off the past
Put away your ashen garments
I've arrayed you in garments of praise.

Throw off your chains, throw off your fetters
I've set you free to dance in liberty
Throw off the things that hold you

I'm calling you to dance in liberty
Whom the Son sets free is free indeed
You will know the Truth and He will set you free
In the name of Jesus I speak Liberty
In the name of Jesus, I say the captives are free
In the name of Jesus I speak freedom
Freedom to dance with me
Freedom to dance unhindered
Freedom to dance in my Glory
Dance the dance of liberty
Dance the dance of deliverance
My revival shall come to you first
That you shall put it on and take it to the rest
You shall dance in rivers of praise
You shall sing songs of deliverance
You shall take up your sword of the Spirit
My word shall go forth from your mouth
From the West to the East to the North to the South
You shall prophesy, "Let my People go, Let my people go,
Let my people go."
You shall see a city set free
There's a River running through your city
Rivers of Praise, Rivers of Worship...
Rivers to set them free!

In the Secret Place

In the Secret Place of the Most High
Is where I find my peace
In the Secret Place of the Most High
I find Your rest
Under the Shadow of the Almighty
I find joy
I find love, I find who I am
And who you are in me.

In the Secret place
Is where I am consumed
As a Living Sacrifice
A Holy, Acceptable, Pleasing, Living sacrifice
It's where I lose who I thought I was
Where I find who you've called me to be.
Where I find You, all of You, All of You
And I lose all of me, All of me in Your Presence.
I find You, and I lose myself in Your Love.
Consumed
Treasured
Captured
Enraptured
Love expressed, Love released
Love exposes me yet Love captures me.

I'm captured by the winds of Your Love
I'm captured by the Breath of Your Spirit
I'm captured in the depth of Your Grace
I'm lost in Your Loving Gaze.
I'm so lost with Heaven's Embrace.

Lost…Selah

Capture me Lord by winds of Your Love
Capture me by the Breath of your Spirit
Capture me in the depth of Your Grace.
Capture me in Your Loving Gaze
Capture me with Heaven's Embrace.
Captured…Selah

For it's in Your Presence I find myself again
For you've called me by name
It's where I discover
It's where I uncover
It's where I believe again
It's where I'm undone.

Undone by extravagant Love
Undone by the wealth of who you are
Undone by Your Magnificence
Undone by Your Majestic Splendor
Undone by how big You are and how small I am
Let me run to your cover…Selah

How I love You
How can I live outside of this place?
For I've come to You and Your Marvelous Grace
I've come to see You face to face.
Eternity has captured my heart
An eternity with You has begun in this place.
Can't imagine a moment outside of this place
Where I in You and You in me collide
Face to face as in a kiss

A Kiss of Eternity
A Kiss, a Romance, a Dance
A place where destinies are created
A place where destinies are initiated
A place where destiny and purpose collide
With Your Will and Your Delight
I lose myself there...Jesus...Jesus...Jesus
I love you...Selah

For I am consumed by Your Fire
I am consumed by Your Passion
I am consumed by Your Love
I am consumed by Your All Consuming Fire
Consumed...Selah

For I have been invited to the place
You said I could come here and get a taste
You have welcomed me with open arms
For Your Glory awaits me here
Glory...Selah

Now that I have tasted of Your Glory
How can I live outside this place?
This place where Your Love meets my Altar
Where I want to hide my face
Yet I find Your Glorious Grace
You've called me here to abide
To live here, reside here, never leave here.
To a place where I abide in You...and You in me
To the place of Your Abiding...Selah

Joy, unspeakable joy in Your Presence
Love, waves of Love crashing over me
Peace, Immeasurable Peace enveloping me
Grace, waves of Your Grace
Waves and waves and
Waves of Your Grace engulfing me...Selah

A place I was created for
Where Eternity fellowships with me
A place You have called me to
A place where I find Your desire
A place where I can go higher
In the realms of Your Spirit
In the warmth of the Hidden place
Where I receive Your Word of Life
Where I conceive Your Seed of Life
Where Your Word is implanted in my spirit
Such an intimate place
Where Your Love has consumed me
Your Love washes over me
Your Love envelopes me
Your Love welcomes to this place...Selah

Sweep me away by Your Love
Sweep me away by Your Spirit
Sweep me away by Your Presence
Sweep me away in Your Heavenly embrace
Face to face...Selah

For You've asked me to dance
You called me by name
You've led me to a place where I lose control

You lead, and I follow as in a dance
You lead, and I follow as in a dance...Selah

The Beauty and the Romance
Of the Bride and Her King
For she is captured within His Gaze
No one else can step in, enter in
Where the Bride and the King enjoy the dance.
All eyes are upon the Bride and the King
She in her loveliness, and He in His majesty
With such ease and such grace
He twirls her in her place
His arms hold her secure
She is safe in His Sweet Embrace
For no one has ever seen this Bride before...Selah

Where did she come from, no one knows
She has arisen from wilderness places
Leaning on Her Beloved
Safe and secure
Beauty arisen from her ashes
Behold the Splendor of the Bride
She reflects His Radiance, His Glory
As she looks into Him and sees who she is,
She is melted into His Embrace.

Behold the Bride in all of her Beauty
Behold the Bride arrayed in Glory
Behold the Bride sealed by a Kiss
Behold the Bride in Her Splendor
No eye has seen, no ear has heard
No mind conceived this moment in Time.

The Bride has prepared herself to meet Her King
A Vision of Loveliness
A Vision of Glory
A spotless and Radiant Bride
A Holy, Acceptable Bride
Without blemish, without wrinkle
She has remained true to His Love
And all of Heaven has awaited this moment.

Where the King and His Bride are revealed
For He has loved her
He has longed for her
He has wooed her
Now He holds His Bride in His Hands
He engages Her in a Kiss, in a dance
In the Fire of His Passion, in His Romance
Behold the Bride and the King in the Dance...Selah

For she has waited in the wings
Wondering if He would pick her
The crowd parts as He walks to her
As He is drawn straight to her
He has extended His hand of Favor
He bowed and asked her for the dance
With her heart in her throat, she whispers
Yes to the Lord and His Dance
Yes to the Lord at His Request
Yes to this Glorious Honor
Yes to the Lord and His Romance...Selah

She has lived all her life for this moment
She has dreamed of this day for so long

And now she finds herself captured
Swept away in a Holy romance
Swept away as in a dance…Selah

No one knows what it took for her to get there
No one knows except the Lord
He called her in spite of her weakness
He called her Accepted, his Beloved.
He called her…Selah

The Flower

A flower once beautiful
Now weakened and frail
Opens its petals one last time
Releasing its Precious seed
She has carefully protected
And in her dying Breath
Says goodbye to all she has known
In her death she produces life.

In her dying moment
She envisions the many
More beautiful who will come after
That she will never behold.
More life did she produce
In death than all of her days
The promise will live on
After she closes her petal
In her last farewell
And wains to the ground.

So is our dying to self
Each day that we die
Produces the promise of more life
More life from our death
Than the sum of all our days
Many more beautiful will come after
Because we chose to die today

Oh that I may die a thousand deaths
God holds precious each one

For God is a farmer
Looking for a harvest of many souls
From those who chose to release in death
To see God's Heart manifested in the earth.
To see God wrap His Arms
Around His Many Beloved
They see the King's Bride
As she is made spotless and irons her clothes

To see God's Love revisit the earth
To see God's Love melt and infuse
The people to Himself
To bring forth such worship
God has never heard before
To hear the Heavenly Worship
Kiss the earth in One Voice

To bring such honor, such Glory
Such praise to our God
To extend God's Love to them
That they will know us by his Love.
To live Heaven out before its time
To touch him so deeply
We will never touch him like we can touch him now.
In our death come praises and adoration
In our trials come exuberant joy
Overwhelming love
As we are pressed out and He is pressed in.
We are His manifested impression on the earth.

Let me die today that His Life will spring forth
Let me die today that those souls

Waiting in the wings may come forth.
Let me stand between Heaven and Hell
That many will never taste that eternity
I die as I live out intercession before my God
Just as Jesus stood between Heaven and Hell
Just as in His death, He produced Life itself
Just as He lived out intercession before the Father
I will take up my cross and follow You.
My Love, My Life, My King, My God.

A Habitation for His Glory

We ask for your habitation
We ask for you to dwell with us
We ask for your habitation
We ask for your Glory.

Let Your Glory come into Your House.
Let Your Glory fill Your Sanctuary.
Let Your Glory come into Your House.
Let Your Glory fill Your Sanctuary.

Unless the Lord builds the House
We labor in vain
So Lord build your House
That Your Glory may come and stay.

The Living Stones cry out
For Your Habitation
On earth as it is in Heaven
As Heaven is filled with Your Glory
So earth is filled with your Glory displayed.

The Living Stones cry out
Come Lord fill your Sanctuary
Refine our love as pure Gold
That we may be Your Habitation
Refine our hearts with love that is pure
That you may come and dwell and never leave.

Prepare ye the habitation
Prepare ye the Way of the Lord
Prepare ye the Habitation
For He inhabits our praise.

Prepare the way of Righteousness
Prepare the way of Peace
He has built the Highway of Holiness
That leads into His Sanctuary.

For He leads in paths of Righteousness
He leads us in paths of Peace
He has paved the way with His Blood
The way to the Father's Heart.

Open the eyes of our understanding
That we may see His Beauty
Open the eyes of our understanding
That we may see His Glory
Open the eyes of our understanding
That we may see His Holiness
Open the eyes of our understanding
That we may be His Habitation.

Let me be your habitation.
Let me be your dwelling place.
Let me be the Temple that your Glory fills
Let me see you face to face.
Lord perfect our praise
That your habitation may come.
Lord refine our worship
Purified, holy, and separated.

Lord come into Your Sanctuary
Lord come into Your Holy Place
Lord bring Your Habitation
Let it indwell our Praise.

Lord we have ceased from our own works
We have entered into your rest
We shall not labor in vain
So Lord come build Your House.

With Living Stones that praise You.
With Living Stones that cry out night and day
With Living Stones of Worship
Purified, refined through Your fire.

Lord send Your Fire
To burn away the chaff
Lord send Your Rain
To wash away the filth of the Daughters of Zion.

Lord send Your Fire
To refine our hearts
Lord send your rain
That washes away our stains.

Send your fire, Send your rain
Make us whole again!
Sanctify us, Separate us,
Purify us, Consecrate us

Lord come and fill Your House with your Presence
Lord come and fill Your House with Your Glory

Lord rebuild the walls of praise
Rebuild the gates of Thanksgiving
Build the inner rooms of worship
Let us come behind the veil to Your Most Holy Place.

Let us see Your Glory
Fill Your Sanctuary
Let us see Your Glory
Come down and fill the Most Holy Place

Immersed in Your Presence
Consumed by Your Fire
Refined as pure gold
Your passion my desire.

Hidden in Your Shelter
Covered by Your Wings
Resting in Your Habitation
Let us become your Dwelling.

Lost in love with you
Dying to love you
Crucified, never to return
Let me die that You may live.

I can't live without Your Presence
I can't live without Your Love
I can't live outside Your Anointing
There's nowhere else for me to go.
So let me dwell with you
You in me, and I in you.

You are the vine, we are your branches
You're abiding in me, and I in you.
Apart from you I can do nothing
But in you, I will bear much fruit.

I've come to the place of Your Abiding
Heart to heart and face to face
Spirit to spirit, private communion
I go to the place of intimacy
Where I felt your heartbeat
Where you whisper words of love to me
Where your strength flows through my veins.

Where I feel your love surround me
Where I feel Your Peace around me
Where I feel your joy within me
Where I feel your strength uphold me.

Where I feel your kiss upon my life
Your love is better than wine
Where I feel your heavenly embrace
Where I am connected to the vine.

You in me, and I in you.
Abide in me and I in you.
In sweet communion
And intimate fellowship
You are altogether lovely.
Abide in me and I in you
Your abiding is better than life.

Let me lose myself here
In the place of Your Abiding
Let me die in your arms of Love
For I'm dying to stay here.

Let us walk in the garden
That you may inspect the fruit
Wash me with the Water of Your Word
Cleanse me and nourish me
That I may bear your Fruit.

Come away with me awhile
To the place that I've prepared for you
That you may know my voice
That you may rest on my heartbeat.

Come and create a habitation
Come and fill my heart
Come and fill your Temple
With the Cloud of Your Glory.

Come and dwell Lord,
Come and dwell with me
Come and dwell Lord
Come and fill your Sanctuary
Come and dwell with me Lord
Come and fill me with Your Glory.

Come and abide Lord
Come and abide in me.
Come and abide Lord, I in you and you in me.
I've come to the place

Of Your Secret Abiding
I've come to the place
Where there is no hiding from you.
I've come to the place
Of sweet surrender
Of your warm embrace
Of Heaven's Encounter.

Your deep calls to my deep
Come with me and you shall see
Things you can't imagine
Things you can't even dream.
Things you've never seen
I'm opening the door to your understanding
I've given you the keys to mysteries untold
It is where I am
Where I unlock your heart.

There shall be no separation
Between you and me in this place
Come abide with me
You shall see my face.

Be filled with my Strength
Come know my grace
My tender mercies are new
To cover your life.
Come stay with me
For I've called you my Bride, my Wife.

Bone of my Bone,
Flesh of Flesh
Spirit of my Spirit
Heart after my own Heart.

You feel my Words
You feel my Love
You feel my Strength
It's all available to you here.

I will unlock you
My sister, My Bride
That all I've put in you
Shall be released
Like floods of many waters
Like a desert with many streams
Like rivers of pure worship
Flowing from you to me.

Unlock me, my Love
For you hold the Key
The Key of My Release
In Sweet ecstasy.

Create in me a Holy Habitation
Create in me a clean heart of purity
Create in me your private Sanctuary
Where I may dine in the Presence of My King.

The Key of Wisdom
The Key of Prophecy
The Key of Understanding

The Key of Revelation
The Key of Your Gifting
The Key of Your Callings
The Key of Your Anointing
The Key of Promotion.

You have given me the keys to your Heart
And I shall give you the keys to my Habitation
I shall pour forth my plans through my Spirit
I shall build my house by My Hands.

I shall open these hidden doors that you can't see
And I shall shut those doors to the enemy
I shall wash those inner rooms with my precious blood
I shall purify them with my precious love.

The Door of Your Heart

Take me Lord, I'll go there with you
Take me Lord, I'm dying to love you
Take me to your secret place
The place of your abiding Love
And your warm embrace
Show me the depths of your heart
I am yours, I am set apart
I'm dying to know you
I'm dying to love you
Let me die more that I may go through that door.

The door to your heart
The door to your unfailing love
That cries out for your lost ones
The door of your heart
That leads to revival
Unless you give me your love for them
I can't love them like you do.
Unless you give me your tears
I can't cry for them like you
Unless you give me your compassion
I can't heal them like you did
For you were moved with compassion
Compassion moved your hand to show them
Your compassion showed your love
Your power and demonstration
Accompanied by Love
Seek Him while He may be found
Knock and the door will be opened to you.

Lord, let me cry for the lost like you do
Let me cry your tears for the dying
Let me be moved by your compassion
Let your hand reach through me to heal them
Lord, demonstrate your love to this lost world
In power, in wonder by your Spirit
Lord create a habitation
A habitation for your Glory.
A dwelling place among your people
An atmosphere where you display your compassion
A sanctuary of your healing.

I approach boldly your Throne of Grace
That I may obtain mercy in my time of need
I ask boldly on their behalf
That they may receive your compassion
That they may receive salvation
That they may receive life and not death
Your deliverance and your healing
That you may bring forth your revival
That you may display your Glory
That Heaven and earth shall join in one voice
To sing Hallelujah to the Lamb
To adorn you with praise
To clothe you in our worship
To anoint your feet and your head as well
With the oil of worship that flows from our hearts.

To cover You who sits on the Throne
With our love and adoration
To bless you with something of worth
That touches you so deeply.

Let the High Praises of all the Saints
Rise to your ear
Let your servants ascribe to you
Glory, Honor, Strength, and Power
For there are no other gods before you
There is none like You!

Let the weight of Your Glory
Descend on us.
Let the Light of Your Glory
Rise within us.
Let your Power and Authority
Manifest in us.
For Your Name's sake
Save the lost and dying
For Your Heart's sake
Bring revival to them
For Your Word's sake
Make the dying live again

We ask for your Rivers of Revival
Flood our hearts
Flood your Sanctuary
Flood this city
Flood this nation
Flood this world with your Revival
And Your Glory
Let Your River flow from Your Heart
Let it go forth to the nations
It's not for us that we ask
Only you can bring alive that which is dying.

We speak to the dry dead bones in this city
We say rise up and dance in His Glory
We speak to dry and weary places
We say rise up in His Strength and Salvation.

No Greater Love

He is my Joy, He is my Life
He is my husband, I am His wife
He is the King, I am His Queen
He is the Bridegroom, I am His Bride
That is who I am in Christ
I am His Queen, I am His Wife
I am His Body, I am His Bride.

For greater love has no man
Than to lay down his life for me
He died for me that I may live
He'd rather die than live without me.

That's why I love Him
For there is no greater Love than his
That's why I must know Him
That He may come forth in this life I live.

Lord I die that You may live.
I decrease that you may increase.
No greater love than that of the Son
He laid his life down for His Bride
No greater love than this
That He laid his life down for her.

I have the right to sign on His Blank Check
It's signed in Jesus Name
All that I ask for will be mine
I ask for this in Jesus name.

I ask for His Agape Love
I ask for His Cleansing Blood
I ask for depths and realms I cannot know
I ask that the dead shall live again
I ask that blind eyes shall see
I ask that the lame shall walk again
I ask that deaf ears shall hear again

I ask that your river flow to the sea
Of lost humanity in this city
I ask for your Glory to dwell and never leave
I ask for revival
I ask for this city
I ask for salvation of every man, woman and child
That none shall die, but all shall live
We're standing between Heaven and Hell
Not willing that any should perish
For this is the will of the Father
That not one shall die.
That all will come to the Son
That will look upon him and bow
That not one shall be lost.

Can you see the Lamb?
He is high and lifted up
Can you see the Lamb?
Look upon Him and live.
He shall draw all men unto His side
He is calling forth His Bride
He is coming to get her
To bring her unto Himself.

Come all you who are weary
Come all who are heavy laden
Look upon Him and live
He will give you His Rest.

Holy, Holy is the Lord
Holy, Holy is the Lamb
Holy is the Lord God Almighty
Who was and is and is to come.

Let Heavenly Angels come before
Let Beloved saints sing and adore
King of Kings and Lord of Lords
Let us cover Him upon the Throne.
As a haze of fragrant worship
As a covering of adoration
Wrapped in the Blanket of Our Love
Adorned in His Glory.

He is crowned with many crowns
His Name is Faithful and True
He steps from his Throne to His White Horse
His enemies to pursue.
He is calling forth His Army
He's calling forth those to ride with Him
He's raising up His Army
They shall ride upon the Wind.

They shall soar upon His Breath
They shall soar as mighty eagles
They shall declare the glories of their King
Unto the very nations.

He's calling forth his chosen ones
That they may bow before His Throne
Then arise in the fullness of his Power
In great authority.

They will go where He shall send them
To the four corners of the earth
To carry forth his Revival Child
Revival of Worship we have birthed.

He is the King of Glory
Great with Power and Authority
He has come to do His Father's Will
That all may look to Him and live.

All of creation groans for him
All of creation longs for Him
Through his Bride, He will step into the earth
All that was lost shall come to Him.

Waves and waves of His Glory shall wash over her
Waves and waves of His Love shall consume her.
Cleanse her, make her spotless
Make her white as snow.
Draw her unto Him
That His Love she may know.

Take me Lord where I cannot go
Take me Lord where I have never known
Unless you lead me there
Where You go, I will follow.

Shall We Dance?

This is the original poem from which The Last Dance was birthed.

Shall we dance with the Lord of our lives?
Shall we dance with the Lord our King?
Lord you take the lead and we will follow
Lead us Lord in the dance of our lives
Lead us Lord as we waltz down the Path of Life
Lead us Lord, our foot in step with yours
Shall we dance with our Lover, our King?
Shall we live our life in sync with your heartbeat?
This is the rhythm of our dance
As you go, we shall follow
Lord you are in the lead.
We are swept away by your Love
We are swept away in your dance
Shall we dance?

Sweep me away by winds of Your Love
Sweep me away by winds of Your Heart
Take me there my Lord, take me there.
Time stands still when I'm with you
I'm so lost in your loving arms
With my eyes fixed on yours
I'm lost in your eternal loving eyes.
So lost…

I trust you as you lead me
One step at a time
I hear the rhythm of your Heartbeat in my ear.
The sound has become deafening

You have beautifully adorned me as Your Queen.
You are arrayed in Majesty, my King
There's no else around, just you and me
An intimate dance with my Love, the King.
I'm so in love, lost in love with you
This is where I lose my life
Right here in your arms.
I have died and gone to Heaven
These moments stand for eternity
Where the Bride waltzes with Her King
No one else can step in.
No one dares approach the Bride and Her King
Her heart beats passionately within her
She's dancing with the one she has longed for
She can think of nothing else but Him
For He is arrayed in Splendor
Her heart is melting into His…

She feels the Love he has had for her
An all consuming passionate fire
She is captured by His Love
She can't believe she is dancing with Him
Her heart has waited for this very moment
He whispers beautiful words of Love to her
As he dances with her.

The King is enthralled with her beauty
For He has longed for this dance as well
His Heart has swelled with his Mighty Love
For her as he leads her in the Dance.
All she can is "I love you, my Lord, I love you…"

Shall I dance with the Lord of my life?
Shall I dance with the Lord my King?
Shall I dance with the One
Who has loved me for all eternity?
Shall I dance with the One who has conquered me
By His Great Love?

I am my lover's and He is mine
I am His Beloved.
Then He stops the Dance for a moment
And warms me with His Embrace
He kisses me with the kisses of His Mouth
I can't bear to leave this place
Where I am with Him
A time of intimacy with my King.

BRIDE SONGS
SERENADES
of the
Heart

Come Away With Me

"Come Away With Me" is a romantic call from the King to His Bride, a conversation between the Bride and Her King. Prepare to respond to his gentle whisper to come away for awhile...

The Lord's Call:
Come away my Love to a place I've prepared for you.
Come away my Bride, there are things I want to show you.
Let me wash away your sorrow
Let me heal your brokenness
Come away with me, I'll wait for you here.
Come away with me, I'll wait for you here.

The Lord's Call:
Come away my Love, let me shelter you from the cold.
The world has bruised you so and I feel your heartbreak.
Let me bring you to the place where all you see is me.
Come away my child, I'll wait for you here.
Come away my child, I'll wait for you here.

My Response:
Let me come with you to a place you've made for me.
Let me come with you there are things you need to show me.
Lord wash away my sorrow
Lord heal my brokenness
Let me come with you, I'll wait for you here
Let me come with you, I'll wait for you here

My Response:

Let me come with you Lord shelter me from the cold
The world has bruised me so and I know you feel my
heartbreak.
Lord bring me to the place where all I see is you
Let me come away with you, I'll wait for you here.
Let me come away with you, I'll wait for you here.

The Last Dance

The Song, "The Last Dance" was originally written with my sister Rene in mind, as she loved to dance and this was a song of romance, about the dance. Beautiful cello solo at the end by Max Dyer compliment the beautiful melodies within the vocals. Prepare to be swept off your feet...

Shall I dance with the love of my life
Shall I dance, you've put stars in my eyes
Shall I dance with my love, my king
I shall follow, but you shall lead
You're the one I've longed for
I never dreamed that you could be
The one I dance with for all eternity.

I have waited all my life for this moment
My heart is stirred as time stands still
I have found my love for a lifetime
I lose myself as the music swells

Shall I dance with the love of my life
Shall I dance, you've put stars in my eyes
Shall I dance with my love, my king
I shall follow, but you shall lead
You're the one I've longed for
I never dreamed that you could be
The one I dance with for all eternity.

You've rescued my heart from loneliness
I look into your eyes of love for me

I have tasted a piece of Heaven
You have swept me away, now my heart is free

Shall I dance with the love of my life
Shall I dance, you've put stars in my eyes
Shall I dance with my love, my king
I shall follow, but you shall lead
You're the one I've longed for
I never dreamed that you could be
The one I dance with for all eternity.

Then Jesus leads me to a place I've never been
With a bow and a kiss He takes my hand
Places it in yours, my earthly king, and He says,
"My love, I've saved the last dance for you in eternity."

Shall I dance with the love of my life
Shall I dance, you've put stars in my eyes
Shall I dance with my love, my king
I shall follow, but you shall lead
You're the one I've longed for
I never dreamed that you could be
The one I dance with for all eternity.

A Lady and Her King

"A Lady and Her King" is an intimate worship song that was birthed out of my relationship with the Lord Jesus in the Secret Place. I believe I have lived each verse in seasons, and that this song is a prophetic call to the Body of Christ to come into a deeper intimacy with the Lord. Be prepared to be swept away in His Heavenly Embrace. Featuring Max Dyer on cello which represents the tenor "Voice of the Lord Jesus," and Don Pope on soprano sax which represents the "Voice of the Bride." This is my signature song, one I have carried with me for over a decade, and represents my ministry, Bride Song Ministries, and the center of my focus, personal intimate worship in the Throne Room of Heaven, the Secret Place, the Holy of Holies.

How He moves me like waves upon the sea.
Rivers of peace and mercy.
His love engulfs me and I'm lost for a time
That's when His heart joins mine.
I lose myself in His Love for me,
So tender and satisfying.
Just a lady and her King.

Broken and bruised I come to Him.
With open arms He receives me.
Though I have nothing to give Him.
His blood, it covers me.
Through eyes of love, He calls me.
He wipes my tears and He shelters me.
Just a lady and her King.

Such Glory and Honor are His alone.
With Splendor and Majesty on His Throne.
How could He love me as His own?
He says, "Child, don't you know the truth?
I loved you so much I died for you."

How You move me like waves upon the sea.
Rivers of peace and mercy.
Your love engulfs me and I'm lost for a time
That's when Your heart joins mine.
I lose myself in Your Love for me,
So tender and satisfying.
Just a lady and her King.

Song of Solomon

"Song of Solomon" was a bride song originally written for a friend's wedding. Taken from scripture, this song depicts the conversation between the Bride and the King, and the intimacy between the Bridegroom and His Bride. Beautiful melodies of flute and saxophone bring the conversations to life!

He comes at night and knocks upon my heart's door
He's altogether lovely standing there
I gaze upon the one my heart has longed for
My Savior, My Love, My Life
My Savior, My Love, My Life

He whispers words of love I have never heard
My heart melts within me at His Voice
Come away with me awhile and share my love
Beloved, My Love, My Life
Beloved, My Love, My Life

My Love, My Joy, My Heart, My King
Jesus, You are everything
My adoring worship I will Bring
My loving praises I will sing (Repeat)

You come at night and knock upon my heart's door
You're altogether lovely standing there
I gaze upon the one my heart has longed for
My Savior, My Love, My Life
My Savior, My Love, My Life

You whisper words of love I have never heard
My heart melts within me at Your Voice
Come away with me awhile and share my love
Beloved, My Love, My Life
Beloved, My Love, My Life

I've Never Loved Like This

"I've Never Loved Like This" is one of the most intimate and hauntingly beautiful of the Bride Songs, which expresses the longing of the Bride to be with the King. My prayer is that this song would usher you into an encounter with the Lord Jesus.

Jesus, You're my Knight in shining armor
You're the armor I wear by night.
You're the righteousness I long for
The life I live by faith, not sight.

The Holy Comforter when I distress
My Constant Redeemer when I transgress.
Lord, I bow before You now
I am humbled by Your Grace.

Your Beauty and Holiness astound me
How Your Love and mercy found me.
You're the standard I live up to (attain to)
You're the Word of Life I cling to.

The Holy Comforter when I distress
My Constant Redeemer when I transgress.
Lord, I bow before You now,
In worshipful embrace.

The gentle touch of a lover's kiss,
The sweet caress of Your Holiness.
I long to hear my Savior's voice
I've never loved like this. Jesus, how I love You.

The Holy Comforter when I distress
My Constant Redeemer when I transgress.
Lord, I bow before You now,
In worshipful embrace.

Unless You Come

"Unless You Come" is a bride song written the day after I returned from Cape Town, South Africa, in essence a Bride Song from South Africa. This was a cry of my heart for this country and for the people who longed for their King. The Spirit and the Bride say "Come, Lord Jesus, Come!"

How I need your Presence
How I need for You to come
Lord bring your Fresh Fire
Bring us into your Holy Desire

Unless You come with Your Majesty
Your Power and Authority
You're clothing us as Royalty
Unless You come
Unless You come

Lord I've come for just a taste
Longing for Heaven's embrace
Lord I want to look into Your face
I want to feel the rains of Glory and Grace

Unless You come with Your Majesty
Your Power and Authority
You're clothing us as Royalty
Unless You come
Unless You come

Blessed are the Pure in Heart
Blessed for they shall see their God
Blessed are the Pure in Heart
For they shall see their God
As He comes, As He comes,
As He comes for them.

Unless You come with Your Majesty
Your Power and Authority
You're clothing us as Royalty
Unless You come
Unless You come

The Two Shall Be One

Flesh of my flesh, bone of my bone
They who were two now have become one.
When I come from the place of the abiding
It is no longer two but only one.
Spirit of my spirit, I in you, you in me.
Spirit of my spirit, the two shall be one.

Your spirit infused into my spirit
My spirit infused into you
There's no degree of separation between you and me.
You cannot tell where one begins and the other ends
Infusion, your spirit infused with mine.
Infusion, my spirit infused with yours.
Let us be one, that I may know the Father's Love.
One in spirit, one in truth
One in spirit, one in truth
I come to the place of your abiding Love
Let us leave here as one.

Let Your Glory be infused into our spirits.
Let us glory in Your Presence.
Let us dwell there and never leave
For we are one in Your Glory
Your Glory goes with us.
I must die to stay in this place
I must die to meet you face to face
I must die to stay here with You.

Awesome Love

Holy Love, Beautiful Love
His Grace and Mercy extended to me
Oh, what an awesome Love.
Holy Love, Tender Love
To know His Love this side of Heaven
Oh, what an awesome Love
Oh what an awesome Love.

By Jesus' stripes, he healed me
By His sacrifice, He saved me.
Wounded and bruised for my transgression
Oh, what an awesome Love.
Oh, what an awesome Love.

Holy Love, Beautiful Love
His Grace and Mercy extended to me
Oh, what an awesome Love.
Holy Love, Tender Love
To know His Love this side of Heaven
Oh, what an awesome Love
Oh what an awesome Love.

Take Me All the Way with You

Jesus take me all the way with you
Jesus take me all the way with you.
To deeper depths than I have ever known
Higher heights than I could ever go
Unless you lead me there, where you go I will follow
So take me all the way with you,
Jesus, take me all the way.

Lord, I ask though none dare ask of you to ever go this far
Lord, I'm seeking you with all my heart
I long to know just who You are
Lord, I'm knocking on this door that few could ever hope to find
So take me to Your secret place,
This intimate place of Your Abiding Love.

Jesus take me all the way with you
Jesus take me all the way with you.
To deeper depths than I have ever known
Higher heights than I could ever go
Unless you lead me there, where you go I will follow
So take me all the way with you,
Jesus, take me all the way.

Lord, I ask though none dare ask of you to ever go this far
Lord, I'm seeking you with all my heart
I long to know just who You are
Lord, I'm knocking on this door that few could ever hope to
find. So take me to Your secret place,
This intimate place of Your Abiding Love.

THRONE ROOM

Worship

Sing Hallelujah to the Lamb

My sister Karen Semones and I were worshiping together, I was sitting at the piano, and she was seated next to me. Karen then entered into a vision, and what she saw, I wrote the lyrics, melody and arrangement within about 10 minutes. It was a very powerful time and we believe this song was birthed from Heaven.

I see the Lord, seated high upon His Throne
Surrounded by His Splendor and Majesty alone.
I see His face, his smile is beaming His Glory and Grace
Come into the warmth of His sheltering embrace.

Sing Hallelujah, Hallelujah,
Sing Hallelujah to the Lamb.
Sing Hallelujah, Hallelujah
Sing Hallelujah to the Lamb.

Jesus says "Come," with his arms wide open for us.
Come and share His intimate touch, His Presence.
I hear His name, I feel His Power flood my soul.
His Love consumes my all, He's the only One enthroned.

Sing Hallelujah, Hallelujah,
Sing Hallelujah to the Lamb. Repeat
Sing Glory to Him, Glory to Him
Sing Glory to the Lamb of God. Repeat

I see the Lord, seated high upon His Throne
Surrounded by His Splendor and Majesty alone.
I see His face, His smile is beaming His Glory and Grace
Come into the warmth of His sheltering embrace.

The Place of Your Glory

You're my hiding place, let me hide in You.
In the cleft of Your Rock
Covered by Your Hand
Let Your Goodness pass before me
As you unfold your plan for me.

You take me by the hand
And you cause me to stand
Where storms used to rage against me.
To the Place of Your Glory
To the Place of Your Glory.

You're my resting place, let me rest in You.
In the cleft of Your Rock
Covered by Your Hand
Let Your Goodness pass before me
As you unveil Your Love and tender mercy.

You take me by the hand
And you cause me to stand
Where storms used to rage against me.
To the Place of Your Glory
To the Place of Your Glory.

In our secret place, where I see Your face
I am changed into Your Glory
I know the thrill when time stands still
You are changing me for Your Glory.

Life and Breath to Me

Your Love purchased me, Your Blood redeemed
You called me child and set me free
My spirit cries out for more of You
Lord, You are Life and Breath to me.

You see me through your Eyes of tender mercy
Your perfect Peace, it shelters me
Rivers of joy and blessings follow
Lord, You are Life and Breath to me.

I see your Mighty Hand displayed
Your awesome Presence, it remains.
I'm thankful for Your Healing Power
It covers me, refreshes me this very hour.
I thank you, I love you Jesus.

I trust Your sovereign Hand, when I don't understand.
Your faithfulness I see
I will praise and love You for all eternity
Lord, You are Life and Breath to me.

I see your Mighty Hand displayed
Your awesome Presence, it remains.
I'm thankful for Your Healing Power
It covers me, refreshes me this very hour.
I thank you, I love you Jesus.

The Lamb of God

Who You are, we want to know Your Love
We want to bless the Lamb of God
We love you Lord, for we shall behold
The precious Lamb of God.

Glory to the Lamb of God
Exalted is His Name over all.
Glory to the Lamb of God
Exalted is His Name over all.
How wondrous in His Grace.
We bless his Holy Name.
Jesus, Jesus, Jesus, the Lamb of God.

Who You are, we want to know Your Heart
We want to love you with our lives.
We love you Lord, for we shall behold
The risen Son of God.

Glory to the Lamb of God
Exalted is His Name over all.
Glory to the Lamb of God
Exalted is His Name over all.
How wondrous in His Grace.
We bless his Holy Name.
Jesus, Jesus, Jesus, the Lamb of God.

Love Song to the Father

Father I sing a love song to You
For words can't express how I'm touched by You
For you are the Love that I feel in my heart
And I shall remain unto you set apart
To love you, to worship you, to adore you
For you are the song in my heart.

With your kind of Love, Jesus loved You.
He laid His life down to bring us to You
For you were the Love that He felt in His Heart
As He suffered and died, the Lamb set apart
To love You, to worship You, to adore You.
For You were the song in His Heart.

His Blood paved a path to Your Heart
How we long to embrace our Father's Heart.

Father we come as your chosen ones
To lay our lives down before Your Throne
For You are the love that we feel in our hearts
And we shall remain unto you set apart
To love you, to worship you, to adore you
For you are the song in our hearts.

His Blood paved a path to Your Heart
How we long to embrace our Father's Heart.

Rivers

Rivers of my Grace, Rivers of my Love
Going forth from here to the nations
Oh the river is rising
Past the ankle, past the knees
Past the loins of birthing
All that is dead shall live again
See my River is rising.

It's coming, it's coming, it's coming
I see My River rising
Don't stand by the bank to watch it pass by
Come out into the deep with me.
Come out into the deep with me.

Rivers of Revival, Rivers of My Glory
Let my waves wash over you
Waves of Glory, Waves of Revival
Crashing over you.

Get ready, get ready, get ready
It's coming, it's coming, it's coming
I said It would, I said it would
Now look around it's here.

Get ready to dance as David did
When He delivered the Ark of My Presence
You are the arks of my Presence
I will cause you to dance like David did.

Adoration

Adoration is the oldest song of this compilation of worship songs birthed in March of 2000. This was one of the songs that propelled me into the Secret Place and into the adoration of the Holy Spirit, the Son Jesus Christ and My Father Abba Father.

Jesus, Jesus, Jesus we need you.
Jesus, Jesus, Jesus, we love you
For you are Holy.
You are Lovely. You are Worthy.
My Jesus I love you, My Jesus I adore you.

Holy Spirit, Precious Spirit, Holy Spirit, we need you.
Holy Spirit, Precious Spirit, Holy Spirit, we bless you.
For you are our Comforter.
You are our Teacher.
You are our Welcomed Guest.
We bless you Holy Spirit, we honor you.

Holy Father, Abba Father, Holy Father, we worship you.
Holy Father, Abba Father, Holy Father, we love you.
For you are Holy.
You are Glory. You are Worthy.
We honor you Precious Father, we love you our Father.

Jesus, Jesus, Jesus we need you.
Jesus, Jesus, Jesus, we love you
For you are Holy.
You are Lovely. You are Worthy.
My Jesus I love you, My Jesus I adore you.

Come

This is a simple prayer for the Three in One Living God to come and inhabit my praise and envelope the Secret Place with me, a desperate cry for His Presence.

Spirit come, Spirit come, Holy Spirit of the Lord
Want to see, want to see the Glory from the Throne
Let your fire, let your oil flow down on me
Saturate me now with your anointing.

Jesus come, Jesus come, the Lover of my soul
Want to see, want to see the Glory from Your Throne.
Cleanse me now with your precious blood upon me.
Let me feel your passion rise within me.

Father come, Father come, let Your Will on earth be done,
Want to see, want to see, the Glory from Your Throne.
I worship you, I honor you for you are Holy.
I lay my life in your hands for you are worthy.

Spirit come, Jesus come, Father come into this place.
Want to see, want to feel, want to know your warm embrace.
Praise your name, I bless your name for you are lovely
I will kiss your precious face with my worship.

I love you Lord, I love you Lord, I want to know your love.
I need your touch, I need your touch, I can never get enough
You're my Life, You're my Joy, You are my King
Lord of Life, Lord of Love, Lord of everything.

To Live in my Father's Love

To live in my Father's Love
To bask in Your Presence
And discover a full revelation of who You are.

To know you more and more
To love you deeper and deeper
To trust you so completely
To worship only you.

The Love of my Father
That wraps my heart completely
The Love of my Father
That penetrates my brokenness
The Love of my Father
That runs after me
And never stops to find me.
The Father's Love that sacrificed all
That I may dwell forever in my Father's Love.
In my Father's Love.

There are many rooms in my Father's Heart.
There are secret rooms of my Father's Love
Knock and the door shall be opened
To that deepest place in His Heart.

The Love of my Father
That wraps my heart completely
The Love of my Father
That penetrates my brokenness
The Love of my Father

That runs after me
And never stops to find me.
The Father's Love that sacrificed all
That I may dwell forever in my Father's Love.
In my Father's Love.

I want to go there…
I want to live there…
Jesus said, "I'm preparing a place for you
That where I am there you may be also."

I am in the Father
The Father is in me.
Let them know the father's Love for them
It is found in Your Heart…in Me.

Let the Heart of the Father
Be opened to His Child
Let the Father's Heart be manifest
And fully known in the earth.

The Love of my Father
That wraps my heart completely
The Love of my Father
That penetrates my brokenness
The Love of my Father
That runs after me
And never stops to find me.
The Father's Love that sacrificed all
That I may dwell forever in my Father's Love.
In my Father's Love.

Conquered by Your Love

I'm justified by faith
In the One that I love
You've washed away my stains
Lord, I'm conquered by Your Love

You've drawn me to your side
You called me Beloved Bride
I've never felt so alive
Lord, I'm conquered by Your Love.

You've touched me with Your Holiness
Consumed me with Your Fiery Love
Embraced me with Your Holy Kiss
I'm conquered by Your Love.
Oh Your Presence captures me
And I am lost for such a time
The Memories of a time gone past
Full circle aged like sweet wine.

Glory to the Lamb

*Glory to the Lamb is a deeply personal worship song written in
2002.*

Glory to the Lamb of God
Exalted is His Name over all!
Glory to the Lamb of God
Exalted is His Name over all!
How wondrous is His Grace!
We bless His Holy Name!
Jesus, Jesus, Jesus, the Lamb of God!

Ascribe to the Lord

Ascribe to the Lord
He is Worthy of Glory
Ascribe to the Lord
The Honor due His Name.
Ascribe to the Lord
He is Worthy of All Praise
Ascribe to the Lord
And praise His Holy Name!

Declare the Mighty Works
Of our Lord and Savior
Declare the Mighty Works
Of His Prophetic Word going forth
Declare the Mighty Works
Of the Mighty Holy Spirit
Declare the Mighty Work
Of His Promised Word.

Ascribe to the Lord
He is Worthy of Glory
Ascribe to the Lord
The Honor due His Name.
Ascribe to the Lord
He is Worthy of All Praise
Ascribe to the Lord
And praise His Holy Name!

INTIMATE SONGS
from the
SECRET
Place

He Who Dwells (Psalm 91)

He who dwells comes directly from Psalm 91 and is a deep reflection of my resting place with the Lord. This song just flowed out of my personal worship in 2002.

He who dwells in the shelter of the Most High
Will rest in the shadow of the Almighty
He who dwells in the shelter of the Most High
Will rest in the shadow of the Almighty

I will say of the Lord, "He is my refuge."
I will say of the Lord, "He is my fortress."
I will say, "He is my God in whom I trust."
I will dwell with Him and rest in His wings.

He who dwells in the shelter of the Most High
Will rest in the shadow of the Almighty
He who dwells in the shelter of the Most High
Will rest in the shadow of the Almighty

I will say of you Lord, "You are my refuge."
I will say of you Lord, "You are my fortress.'
I will say, "You are my God in whom I trust."
I will dwell with you and rest in your wings.

I have ceased from my own works
And I will enter Your rest
I have laid my burdens down
And I will enter Your Peace
I shall dwell with You
And rest in Your peace.

Take the Broken Parts

This song comes from a deep and broken place as I surveyed the broken pieces of my life in 2003. This song echoes the song of David who cried in the arms of the Lord many times. This song wells up from a heart of David that just wants to worship the Lord in spite of all circumstances.

Lord, take the broken parts
The remnants of my broken heart
Lord I give a fragrant offering
Let it be pleasing unto you.

Lord, turn not your eyes from me
Hear my cries, remember me
I lay my life down at your feet
I cling to your tender mercy.

Lord take every part
Bring me Jesus to where you are
With silver strands, redeem my heart.
Bring Glory to Your Name.

Lord, take the broken parts
The remnants of my broken heart
Lord I give a fragrant offering
Let it be pleasing unto you.

I Will Trust You

I wrote this song in 2003 through very difficult times emotionally, when my world seemed to be closing in and my dreams were dashed. Even in the midst of that place this song came forth as worship even when I did not understand the things that were happening around me. Sometimes you just have to hold onto the hand that holds you and trust the Love that you have known and the Goodness of your Lord.

I will trust you when I am afraid
And I will behold you when darkness blinds my way
Jesus, I worship you, Jesus I worship You.
I will trust you when I've lost my way
And I will seek you in the stillness of this place
Jesus I worship you, Jesus I worship you.

Jesus, Jesus, Redeemer, Precious Lord,
Jesus, My Jesus, No one could take your place,
For you have shown me your Glory and Grace.

I will trust you when I am afraid
And I will behold you when darkness blinds my way
Jesus, I worship you, Jesus I worship You.
I will trust you when I've lost my way
And I will seek you in the stillness of this place
Jesus I worship you, Jesus I worship you.

Jesus, Jesus, Redeemer, Precious Lord,
Jesus, My Jesus, No one could take your place,
For you have shown me your Glory and Grace.

I Feel Jesus in This Place

I wrote this song in 2004 during difficult times. I remember being in my bathroom, crying and I could feel this soothing Presence come in and rest with me, and these words and melodies started flowing in response to this beautiful encounter with the Lord. A very precious song that reminds me of the tenderness of the Lord Jesus towards his Beloved.

I feel Jesus in this place
I see Jesus' Glorious face
I feel Jesus' warm embrace
I feel Jesus in this place.

His eyes of love surround me
His loving arms secure me
He's placed my feet upon an immovable rock
For Jesus' Glory He has given to me.

I feel Jesus in this place.
I see Jesus' beaming face.
I feel Jesus' warm embrace surrounding me.
I feel Jesus in this place.

He is clothed with Majesty and Splendor
He is crowned with Glory and Power
He is adorned with Might and the Strength of His Word.
For He has been given the Name above all Names.

I feel Jesus in this place, I see Jesus' radiant face
I feel Jesus' loving embrace surround His people.
I feel Jesus, I feel Jesus, I feel Jesus in This Place!

Alone

I feel so all alone, I need you by my side.
I have nowhere to go and no place to hide.
I used to know Your Touch and felt Your warm embrace.
I heard Your Voice so clearly now I long for just a taste.

But I hear You say You love me
That You could never leave me
If I call Your Name You'll answer from Heaven.
I long to say I love You
That I will never leave You
I call Your name from deep inside my heart.
Jesus I need You so.

Lord take me to the place where we can be as one.
Redeem my straying heart as I return to my first Love.
You say, "Come away with me,
To a place You've never known
Come higher in my Love and deeper as my own.

But I hear You say You love me
That You could never leave me
If I call Your Name You'll answer from Heaven.
I long to say I love You
That I will never leave You
I call Your name from deep inside my heart.
Jesus I need You so.

Be Still and Know

I will sing you praises, for worthy are you
I'll hold on to Your Light to see me through
You are my Father, and I am your child
Nothing could ever keep me from You.

I will rest in Your Love, sheltered from the storm
I am hungry for Your touch, that penetrates my soul
I will worship you right here
Because I know that You are near.
Be still and know that I am God.
He's saying, "Be still and know that I am God.
Be still and know I am Your God."

I will bring my worship, for Holy are you
I'll hold on to Your Light to see me through
You are my Father, and I am your child
Nothing could ever keep me from You.

I will rest in Your Love, sheltered from the storm
I am hungry for Your touch, that consumes my very soul
I will worship you right here
Because I know that You are near.
Be still and know that I am God.
He's saying, "Be still and know that I am God.
Be still and know I am Your God."

For I have not left to swim on your own
For you shall walk across the water
Until I carry you home.
Until I carry you home.
For I have called you my own.

I will rest in Your Love, sheltered from the storm
I am hungry for Your touch, that penetrates my soul
I will worship you right here
Because I know that You are near.
Be still and know that I am God.
He's saying, "Be still and know that I am God.
Be still and know I am Your God."

I give all I am to you
For all you are to me.
I give all I am unto the Great I am.
All my worship, all my praise,
All my love and adoration.
I give all I am unto the Great I am.

Worthy, Worthy is the lamb
Worthy, is the Lamb who was slain for us.
Worthy, Worthy is the lamb
Worthy, is the Lamb who was slain for us. Jesus!

Jesus is My Righteousness

I want to live at the feet of Jesus
That is where I want to stay
To live in the Love that He has for me.
This is where I shall remain.

To live as praise unto my Jesus
A life of worship I shall be
To hear Him, to see Him by faith
Until that day when we shall meet.

With unveiled face I shall behold Him
Such Beauty is His Holiness
As He is so shall I become
For Jesus is My Righteousness.

For He is my badge of Honor
My courage when I'm unsure
For I am a broken vessel
That He has made Holy and Pure.

Tender passionate moments with Jesus
That consume me, overwhelm me.
Holy Exhilaration
His Presence explodes within me.
My constant desire is to be touched by Him
As His Heart becomes Mine, His mind redefines,
His Love so divine transforms my life
Only let Jesus be seen in me.

Dreaming

*In my dream I was singing in perfect rhymes and awakened out of
it to capture some of what I could remember… Beautiful…*

I know just where you are
'Cause He has taken me so far
He is my morning Star!
One day I will be His Wife
With Him I have no strife
He is the Strength of my Life!

He is my Cloud and my Fire
He leads me by day and night
He sings to me of His Desire
I don't walk without Him in my sight.
Every time I think of Him. He is my joy delight
I know that I can't live without Him
I keep Him within my sight.

*To know the height, the depth, the length,
The breadth of Your Love for me
To know the height, the depth, the length,
The breadth of Jesus' Love for me.
Liquid tangible Love pour over me
Consuming, burning Love wash over me.*

Beloved

Lord, you are my refuge and my strength.
And when I pass through this storm,
Hidden in you, kept safe and warm.
I'll rise to my feet to stand in your love for me.

You've cried my tears, You've embraced my pain.
But you would never leave me alone.
You covered my shame, You whispered my Name.
Beloved, I have called you out for my own.

Come unto me and you will find
Rivers of Life. Come now and drink of me.
Come unto me and you will find
Rest for Your soul, come close and you shall see
What I shall do for you, I'm calling you.
I sing my song over you.

Lord, I thank you for carrying me through.
For I shall never be the same.
You stood in my place, you whispered my name.
Beloved I have called you out for my own.

Come unto me and you will find
Rivers of Life. Come now and drink of me.
Come unto me and you will find
Rest for Your soul, come close and you shall see
What I shall do for you, I'm calling you.
I sing my song over you.

For I have called you Mighty,
With Power and Authority.
I call you friend, I call you my child.
I call you loved and you are mine.

Come unto me and you will find
Rivers of Life. Come now and drink of me.
Come unto me and you will find
Rest for Your soul, come close and you shall see
What I shall do for you, I'm calling you.
I sing my song over you.

The Heart of My Presence

The Lord's Invitation
Draw near to the Heart of My Presence
For My Glory is waiting there.
My peace shall light upon your face
As you lay at my feet your care.

I long to immerse you in rivers
That flow from My Spirit, My Heart.
You shall enter my rest, child,
You shall drink from the Love of My Heart.

Let me Heal You in My Presence
For I long to make you whole.
Let me touch you with My Holiness
You shall hunger and thirst,
You shall hunger and thirst
You shall hunger and thirst no more.

My Response at His Invitation
Draw me near to the Heart of Your Presence
For Your Glory is waiting there.
Your peace shall light upon My face
As I lay at Your feet my care.

I long to be immersed in your rivers
That flow from Your Spirit, Your Heart.
For I shall enter Your rest, Lord,
I shall drink from the Love of Your Heart.

Lord, You heal me in Your Presence
For You long to make me whole.
Lord, just touch me with Your Holiness
I shall hunger and thirst,
I shall hunger and thirst
I shall hunger and thirst no more.

Jesus Healer of My Soul

Jesus Healer of my soul
Jesus You make me whole.
Jesus Comforter and Friend
Jesus to You there is no end.

I love You with all I am
Jesus the Mighty Lamb
You laid down Your Life in exchange for mine.
I am Yours Lord, and You are Mine.

I give you my heart, my soul, my mind
Jesus, Your Presence I find.
Your Peace, Your Rest, Your Love Divine
I am yours, you are mine.

Lord, I worship You as Prince of Peace
For You are my Desire.
Consume with me Your Fire again
Lord I worship you as King of Kings.
For You are my Desire.
Consume with me Your Fire again

Where Can I Go?

Where can I go that your gaze doesn't capture me?
Where can I go that your gaze doesn't mesmerize me?
As I long to look in the eyes that love me so
I am lost in Your Loving Gaze.

As you look through me to the depths of my fears
As you look past me to the Beauty I am to become
As you search the depths of my heart
To a love I cannot express
You see me as I am and love me in this place.

I feel your abiding love strengthen me, holding me
For my King is enthralled with my Beauty
I feel your embrace shelter me
I feel your passionate touch
Desperate to pull me to yourself.

As you touch my face and draw me with your gaze
All time melts away as I am lost in your kiss.
Swept away by the intimacy of your embrace
I find where I belong with you face to face
I behold the One who has captured my heart
Everything else loses its meaning
Only this remains
I'm so lost in love with you
Words cannot express what I feel here with you.
My love for you is rekindled
With the fire of Your Spirit

My passion is renewed as I return to love's first kiss
The One I've longed for all my life
Stands before me altogether lovely
The song rises from my spirit
I don't know whether to dance or be still
In this place I have lost my will
To run or hide from you
I am perfected in Your Gaze
I am covered by Your embrace
You are taking me from Glory to Grace
And then to Glory and Grace again.
Abide with me My Love
Stay here with me a little longer
Let love linger while we are here, just you and I
I love you, my Jesus, I love you.

His Heartbeat

As I sit at Your feet and I look into You
I'm in awe of Your Love, eternal and true
As I leave Your Embrace and stand to my feet
Empowered by Your Hand, ready to go for You.

We connect to His Heartbeat
As we march to His drum
Connect to God's power, united as one.
With eyes stayed on You
Our hearts are attuned.
Move us into Your Glory, Oh Lord!

That powerful place where Your Peace covers me
Surrounded by Love, Your Grace and Mercy
By Your Spirit I am led to the battle of life
This place goes with me as I press towards the Prize!

We connect to His Heartbeat
As we march to His drum
Connect to God's power, united as one.
With eyes stayed on You
Our hearts are attuned.
Move us into Your Glory, Oh Lord!

As we march into battle,
What do you think his Drum sounds like?
It is the same sound of His Heartbeat, His Peace.
Breath of God Kiss me
Holy Spirit release your Power and authority
To heal me and deliver me

From the Snares of the enemy!
Oh Holy Spirit come stay with me!
Holy Spirit reveal to me the ways of my Lord
So tenderly the thoughts He has for me.
Holy Spirit lead me to the place where His Glory I finally see!

Rooted and Grounded in His Love

Rooted and grounded in His Love
Established by His Grace
Lifted above all circumstance
As I look upon His Face
I see the Glory of His Grace.

How Jesus loved me
He loved me from the cross
His Love reached through eternity
To heal me and to save me
Deliver and restore me.
To bring me before His Majesty.

Rooted and grounded in His Love
Established by His Grace
Lifted above all circumstance
As I look upon His Face
I see the Glory of His Grace.

The Path of Life

Lord lead my feet to Your path of Life
Let my spirit look up to You
Open my eyes Lord that I may see
The course you have planned for me.

Your light leads me through a darkened place
I shall not stumble because of Your Grace
Lord set my feet on Your grassy plains
By still waters I shall rest
Establish me in my inheritance
That I may live in Your best.

Lord I offer to You a living sacrifice, for all I am is Yours.
Let Your Fire purge away the dross
And make a vessel that is holy and pure.

I give you my heart, my soul, my mind
Jesus Your Presence I find.
Your Peace, Your rest, Your Love Divine
I am Yours Lord and You are mine.

Lord I worship You as Prince of Peace
You are my Holy Desire
Lord I worship you as the Righteous King
Consume me with Your Fire!

The Love of God

To know the height, the depth,
The length, the breadth of Your Love for me.
To know the height, the depth,
The length, the breadth of Your Love for me.
To know the height, the depth,
The length, the breadth of Jesus' Love for me.
Of Your Love in me, of your love in me.

How vast are the seas
Your love extends to me.
You placed the stars so high
So far that I can't see
All I have in me
I give to know Your awesome Love for me
A love so tender, love so pure
I cannot comprehend
A holy love to death endured,
Forever without end.

To know the height, the depth,
The length, the breadth of Your Love for me.
To know the height, the depth,
The length, the breadth of Your Love for me.
To know the height, the depth,
The length, the breadth of Jesus' Love for me.
Of Your Love in me, of your love in me.

You gave your gift to me
Your Son at Calvary
Your heart bled inside
As you watched Him suffer and die.
The perfect sacrifice
His death gave me Your Love and His Life.
A love so tender, love so pure
I cannot comprehend
A holy love to death endured,
Forever without end.

Love is patient, Love is kind,
His Love bears all things.
Envies not, nor is proud,
Thinks no evil thing.
Believes, endures, hopes unseen
The Love of God in me.

Jesus, the Love Song in Me

Lord, be the song of my heart
Breathe in me the breath of Your Love
Create me to be a fragrant melody
Jesus, be the Love Song in me.

Healing River

Let Your Healing River wash over me
Waves of Your Love and tender mercy
Wash me now by Your Cleansing Flood
Of Your Precious Blood, dear Lord.

Let Your Healing Anointing flow over me
Waves of Your Love and tender mercy
Wash me now by Your Cleansing Flood
Of Your Precious Blood, dear Lord.

Let Your Awesome Glory wash over me
Waves of Your Love and tender mercy
Wash me now by Your Cleansing Flood
Of Your Precious Blood, dear Lord.

Let Your Healing River wash over me
Waves of Your Love and tender mercy
Wash me now by Your Cleansing Flood
Of Your Precious Blood, dear Lord.

Come and Drink of My Worship

This song comes from my deep personal worship about 2002. As I reflected about the alabaster jar, I realized I was the broken one and the worship that was spilling out from me was my adoring offering unto him. As painful and difficult as it felt at times, my comfort came that he was pleased in receiving it because He knew the cost and the price I had paid to give it to Him. And it was worthy. And I was accepted by Him.

Come and drink of my worship
Come and taste my adoration
Come and sip of my love for you
For I am poured out like water before you.
Broken and spilled out before you
A fragrant offering unto you,

Prayer of Jabez

Oh, that you would bless me indeed
And enlarge my territory
That Your Hand would be with me.
And that you would keep me from evil
That I may not cause pain.

Lord, bless me, that I may be Your Blessing
There's a hungry world to feed
Let me be the Hands of Jesus
As I praise Your Holy Name.

Jesus, Set me Free

I walk around bruised
Tattered, worn, confused
No one sees my pain at all.
Words that cut like knives
Penetrate inside
Only Jesus hears my call.
But, I, His Beloved, shall stand up this day.
For I, the Accepted, shall rise up and say.

I shall be free, from words of tyranny
I shall be free, from angry words instilled in me.
For I do not receive them.
And I shall not believe them
I break their hold on me.
Jesus set me free.

They walk around bruised
Tattered, worn, confused
No one sees their pain at all.
Words that cut like knives
Penetrate inside
Only Jesus hears their call.
But, they, His Beloved, shall stand up this day.
For they, the Accepted, shall rise up and say.

They shall be free, from words of tyranny
They shall be free, from angry words instilled in them.
For they do not receive them.

And they shall not believe them
You break their hold on them.
Jesus set them free.

The precious blood of Jesus
Heals and restores us
Precious Blood of Jesus
Heal us and restore us.
Precious Blood of Jesus cover me.
Precious Blood of Jesus cover us.

To be Kissed by Him

I want to be lost in the arms of Jesus
I want to be warmed by His Embrace
I want to lose myself in the arms of Jesus
I want to be kissed by Him.

To be kissed by Him
To be kissed by Him
I want to be kissed by Jesus.
To be kissed by Him
To be kissed by Him
To be lost in the embrace of Heaven
To be kissed by Jesus…

DECLARATIONS
of the
Bride

Arise and Shine

Arise and Shine is a song derived from Isaiah 60:1 which is subtitled The Glory of Zion. "Arise, shine, for your light has come, and the Glory of the Lord rises upon you." This song is a prophetic call to the Bride of Christ to rise up and prepare to meet the King of Glory, featuring instruments such as the trumpet which heralds the call to assembly and other prophetic instruments including, cello, saxophone, flute, etc.

Arise and shine for your light has come
Arise and shine for the night is broken
Arise and shine for His Glory's upon you
Arise and shine for the Dawn of the Son

Arise and shine awake from your slumber
Arise and shine lay down your hard labor
Arise and shine for the Glorious Appearing
Arise and shine for your King is coming

Arise oh Bride, Arise oh Bride, Arise oh Bride
Your King is coming!
Arise oh Bride, Arise oh Bride, Arise oh Bride
Your King is coming!

Arise and shine the Bridegroom is coming
Arise and shine He's coming for His Bride
Arise and shine the Bridegroom is rising
Arise and shine, he's rising in his Bride

Arise oh King, Arise oh King, Arise oh King
Rise up in me!

Arise oh King, Arise oh King, Arise oh King
Rise up in me!
Arise oh Bride, Arise oh Bride, Arise oh Bride
Your King is coming!
Arise oh Bride, Arise oh Bride, Arise oh Bride
Your King is coming!

Arise and shine the trumpets are sounding
Arise and shine they're sounding his call
Arise and shine He's raising his army
Arise and shine for the time is now

Arise oh God, Arise oh God, Arise oh God
Rise up in me!
Arise oh God, Arise oh God, Arise oh God
Rise up in me!
Arise oh King, Arise oh King, Arise oh King
Rise up in me!
Arise oh King, Arise oh King, Arise oh King
Rise up in me!

Arise and shine for your light has come
Arise and shine, A new day is dawning
Arise and shine yesterday's over
Arise and shine for the Glorious Appearing

Arise oh King, Arise oh King, Arise oh King
Rise up in me!
Arise oh King, Arise oh King, Arise oh King
Rise up in me!
Arise oh Bride, Arise oh Bride, Arise oh Bride
Your King is coming!

Arise, My Church, Arise

The Lord gave me this song in June of 2000. It was amazing in how I received it, like it was literally a download from Heaven. I have carried this song for over 10 years, awaiting the Lord's timing to release it. The urgency has come to the forefront of this song and the days we are living in. I believe the Lord is waiting for His Church, His Body to Arise in all of the fullness he gave her, in Power and Authority, without spot, wrinkle or blemish. I pray the Body of Christ hears His Voice and responds to His Call, for this is the Hour, this song is now!

I see my people hurting
It grieves my heart to say.
They say they really know me
They're walking their own way.
Enslaved by their love for this world.
I'm calling them out by My Word.

I'm seeking my own who have the heart.
To worship me alone, be set apart.
For those who will walk that line with me,
I'll raise up this hour to lead.

Arise my Bride - You are sleeping from within.
Come alive. Dry bones I cover you with skin.
Clothed with strength and power
I've called you to walk in.
Arise, My Church, Arise.

My Glory I have called for you to be.
My Light in this dark place for them to see.

For those who will learn of My Spirit
They are no longer asleep.

They shall rise up from their ashes.
They shall run and not grow faint.
For My Resurrection Power
Shall raise them by My Name.

Arise, my Bride – You've been sleeping from within.
Come alive. Dry bones I cover you with skin.
Clothed with strength and power
I've called you to walk in.
Arise, My Church, Arise.
Arise, My Church, Arise, My Bride, Arise My Love,
Arise, Arise, Arise, Arise! Arise! Arise!

The Prophet's Cry

Hear the voice of the Bridegroom
Calling from on High
Come up to where I am
And stand by my side
Hear the voice of the Victor
Calling to His Bride
Arise my Church and take your place
My power can't be denied.

For Jesus is coming to take his Place
The Lion of Judah is roaring from his Throne
The lines He has drawn in the sand
The Battle of all times is at Hand
He's jealous for His own!

Hear the sounds of Victory
Hear the voices that long to be free
The King is coming.
To demonstrate His Power
With Rivers of Revival
The Spirit is moving
The trumpets are resounding
His army is advancing
The Church is rising
Clothed in His Authority
Standing in His Victory
The Bride is reviving!

Away with your ashen garments
I've given you garments of praise
Adorned in clothes of My Splendor
Let My Glory fill this place
Let me clothe you in Mantles of Power
With Authority in My Name
For I have called you this hour
With Boldness to proclaim.

For darkness shall not take over you
I have caused My Glory to cover you in this place.
For greater are they that are with us
Than those that our eyes can see
Jesus give us Grace!

Hear the sounds of Victory
Hear the voices that long to be free
The King is coming.
To demonstrate His Power
With Rivers of Revival
The Spirit is moving
The trumpets are resounding
His army is advancing
The Church is rising
Clothed in His Authority
Standing in His Victory
The Bride is reviving!

He is coming to take back His Land
Our Redeemer holds in His Hands the Keys of Revival
The Bride is rising to take her stand
Armies of darkness shall fall at Her Hand.

Hear the sounds of Victory
Hear the voices that long to be free
The King is coming.
To demonstrate His Power
With Rivers of Revival
The Spirit is moving
The trumpets are resounding
His army is advancing
The Church is rising
Clothed in His Authority
Standing in His Victory
The Bride is reviving!

The King is coming! The Spirit is moving!
The Church is rising! The Overcomer is standing!
Apostles are healing! Evangelists are calling
That Jesus is coming!
The Prophets are crying,
"Let my people go!
Let my people go!
Let my people go!"

Arise O Daughter of Zion

Arise, Arise O Daughter of Zion
Put away, put away your ashen garments
Put away the clothes this world put on you
Arise, Arise O Daughter of Zion
Put on your garments of Splendor
Prepare, get ready
You are going to meet Your King

The King is enthralled with your beauty
Awake, Awake O Daughter of Zion
For He clothes her and wraps her in Splendor
He has adorned her in Beauty
She is the beautiful Bride
Fit for His Holy Majesty

He is clothed with Honor
He is clothed with Grace
He is clothed with Glory
He is clothed with Praise
Adorned with Great Humility
Dressed with exaltation
He radiates His Splendor
His Holiness and Majesty

How much less is She?
She is the mere reflection of Her King in His Eyes
She is adorned and prepared
To be presented to Her King

The Holy Spirit is preparing
The Royal Bride to meet her Royal King
Making her spotless
Without wrinkle, without blemish
Making her Beautiful with His light in her eyes.

If He presented Eve to Adam
How much more beautiful shall He present her
The Royal Bride to the Exalted and Risen King?

Shout of the Victor

Jesus said, "Let my people go
Let my people go, let my people go.
Let them go, Let them go, Let them go!
Break free with the shout of the Victor
Break free with a shout of Victory
If the Son has set your free,
Then you are free indeed!
If the Son has set you free,
Then you shout the Victory! Hallelujah!!
I am free…I am free…I am free…
Hallelujah I am free!
Hallelujah we have the Victory!

I am free because Jesus set me free!
Cross over to the other side!
Cross over…cross over to the other side!
I'm walking to the Promised Land,
I'm walking with His Promises in Hand!
He's taking me to a wealthy place
He makes me rich, no sorrow to it!
I will bless His Holy Name!

When you see devils cast out,
The Blind are seeing, the lame are walking
The deaf are hearing
The gospel preached to the poor in spirit
You know the Kingdom is near!
You know His Kingdom is Here!

Let the People Say

Let the people say
Greater is He that is with us
Let the people say
We are well able to take the land
Let the people say
Jesus is our Victory
Let the people say
He will take it back by His Hand

Every knee shall bow
Every tongue confess
That Jesus Christ is Lord
Jesus Christ is Lord over all.

Over our families, over our cities
Over this nation, over His Church
Jesus Christ is Lord in Heaven and in the earth.

Ascribe to the Lord
You are Holy and Righteous
Ascribe to the Lord
Arrayed in Splendor and Majesty
Ascribe to the Lord
You are King over all.

Let the enemy hear that Jesus is coming
The King is taking back His Land
Let the enemy hear The Lord is Mighty in Spirit
Let the enemy hear Jesus Christ is Lord!

Arise in Us

Let the glory of God arise in us
Let the Glory of God arise in us.
Let the Glory of Jesus arise in us.
Let the Glory of the father come down on us.
Let the Glory of Jesus
Kiss the glory of the Father
As in Solomon's day
Let it fill this place.
Let your glory come down
Let the Weight of Your Shekinah Glory cover us
Let your resident Glory stay and never leave.

We ask for your Glory
Let it fill this place
We ask for your Glory
Let it come and never leave.

Let us behold Him
Who sits upon his Throne
Let Him walk among His People
We will worship Him alone.

Let the Light of His Glory arise in us
As He is in this world so shall we be.
Changed from Glory to Glory
Into his very image
Changed from glory to Glory
Into the image of his Son.

Let us make man in our own image
The image of the Son
For I am their Father
And they are my sons.

We are the Sons of God
We shall rise up in power
We are the Sons of God
We shall rise up in Victory

To take back this city
Back from the enemy
To take back this city
From the hand of the enemy.

We have overcome this city
For He has overcome the world.
We have overcome this city
For He has overcome the world.
We are taking back this city
We are walking in the Victory

He is sending forth His Light
Into all the nations
To take back in Victory
What was stolen from Him.

He is sending forth the Light
We are His Light
He is sending forth His Light
Into all the nations.

We are the salt of the earth
He sprinkles on the nations
We are the Salt of the Lord
Seasoned with His Glory and Power.

We have overcome
By His Precious Blood
We have overcome
By the Word of Our Testimony.

We have come to worship you
We have come to give you praise
We have come to bring Honor to the Son
In Whom we love.

Give Honor to the Son
Give Honor to the Son
Give Honor to the One we Love

Open our eyes that we may behold Him
The Lover of our soul
Open our eyes that we may see
The One our hearts adore!
Let us see Him
Let us gaze upon the One our hearts adore!
Let us gaze upon Him for He is lovely
Let us gaze upon Him for He is beautiful

For He is the Wisdom from Above
He is altogether Lovely
He is our salvation
The one that we adore.

He is the Door
Into the Throne Room
He is the Door
That we must walk through.
He is the Vine
We are the Branches
Abide in us and us in You.
That we may bear your fruit.

Take us to the place of Your Abiding
That we may be one in You
Take us to the Place of your Abiding
You in me and I in you.
Let us be one in perfect unity.

You are altogether lovely
I can't bear to leave this place
You are so beautiful
Where I meet with you face to face.

Spirit to spirit
Heart to Heart
Mind of Christ manifest in us.
Make us one in the Son
We are in love with Jesus.
Make us one with the Father
As we are one in the Son.
Make us one with the Father
Let us know His Love for us.
How high, how deep, how far, how wide
Is the Love of Christ for us.
I am the Vine and you are the Branches

Abide in me and I in you
Apart from me you can do nothing
In me, you will bear much fruit.

In the place of Your Abiding, Revival is birthed there
You in me and I in you, Let revival be born here.

We bear the child of promise
We birth the child of revival
I feel the labor pains of intercession
The groanings and moanings of the Spirit
As we bring forth the child of revival
Groanings and moanings of the Spirit
Groaning for the Child
Groaning for the Promise
We're bringing forth Revival.

Moaning and groaning for the lost
Wailing with tears for the dead
Moaning and groaning for the lost
The dead shall live again.

Turn your river to the sea
The sea of lost humanity
Where all that's dead shall live again
See the river's rising.
Past the ankles, past the knees
Past the birthplace of the loins
See it's rising shoulder deep
Let's swim in the River of His Love.

This is where Revival begins
In the Place of Your Abiding
Who I once was shall never be
Only you Jesus arise in me
For I am crucified with Christ
Yet I live, not I but Christ in me.
You have come to set me free
Let my spirit soar with you
As an eagle soars on the breath of Your Spirit
I will rise and soar with you.

I'm dying here to love
In the secret place
Let me die more that I may know you
In the place, the place of Your Abiding.

I have come to love and adore you
Let me know the depths of Your Love
I will rise on eagle's wings
I will know the heights of Your Love.

I will die a thousand deaths
That they will know how long is your love
I will go all the way with you
That millions will know how wide is your love
Your love…That wraps around them
Your love…that surrounds them
Your love that will go farther than they can know
Your love…we are the loving arms that will show
Your love.

How high, how deep,
How far, how wide is the love of Christ.
We say unto this mountain
Be cast into the sea.
We shall crucify this flesh
That we will bring forth a fragrance unto Thee.

Fragrance of our worship
Fragrance that anoints you
The fragrance of our dying
That you may arise with life in us.
I'm dying to love you.
I'm dying to know you.
I'm dying that you may come forth
All of you and none of me.

Jesus arise in me that they may know you
Arise in me that they may love you
Arise in me, I decrease to nothing
Arise in me
That you increase to everything in me.

Sending Forth the Light

All will come and bow down
All must profess
That Jesus Christ is King of Kings
Jesus Christ is Lord of Lords

You're sending forth the Light
To pierce through the darkness
Let your Light arise in me
That you may send me to dispel the darkness.

He's sending forth the Light
Sending forth the Light into the darkness
Sending forth the Light
He's setting the captives free.

For they shall behold Him
The veils of darkness shall be lifted
The veils of blindness shall be rent in two
The grip of the enemy shall be loosened
They shall declare that he is God.

Look upon the One you pierced
Look upon the One you have slain.
Look upon the One at His Right Hand
Look upon Him, He is your King.

For He is high and lifted up
That all may look upon him
He shall draw all men unto Himself
He shall cleanse them from their sin.

For He is your Salvation
He is the Mighty Exclamation
"It is finished, it is done!
Believe upon me, all you who have come."

You provided for Your People
Then you fed the city through Your Son
We ask for your provision
That we may feed this city through Your Son..
We offer up the bread and fish
We ask for your Mighty Blessing
Multiply it from Heaven's Bounty
That the earth receive Your Blessing.

For we are the Hands of Jesus
Offering up the bread and fish
Asking you to pour out a Blessing
According to Heaven's Mercy.

Come Eat from the Lord's Table

Come eat from the Lord's Table
His bounty shall satisfy
Find healing for the disabled
Deliverance to silence their cries
His Peace shall abound
His Love shall be found
His Presence surrounds His Glorious Table
He has an endless supply.

Come eat from the Lord's Table
His bounty shall satisfy
Salvation for the unable
Prosperity that won't run dry.
His Peace shall abound
His Love shall be found
His Presence surrounds His Glorious Table
He has an endless supply.

Come eat from the Lord's Table
His bounty shall satisfy
Find joy for your sorrows
His Grace He shall not deny.
His Peace shall abound
His Love shall be found
His Presence surrounds His Glorious Table
He has an endless supply.

Sing Unto the Lord

Sing unto the Lord a new song of praise
Sing unto the Lord a shout of Victory
We have overcome
We have overcome
By the Blood of the Lamb
And the Word of our testimony
Sing unto the Lord and shout the Victory
Sing unto the Lord and shout the Victory
Sing, Shout, Lift your praises up
Sing, Shout, See the walls come down.
See the Sword of the Lord
That comes from the mouth of the King
See the Sword of the Lord
Cutting off the enemy.

We're going to the Promised Land
Delivered to us by His Hand
We're going to the Promised Land
We are taking our stand.

We take our stand
With our feet upon the Rock
We're taking back the Land
We're going forward and not looking back.

Armed with the Word of the Lord
Armed with our Shield of Faith
Armed with His Precious Blood
Armed with His Sufficient Grace
I take up the Sword of the Spirit

I take up my shield of Faith
I'm covered by His Precious Blood
I stand on His Sufficient Grace

We are armed with His Power
We are armed with His Authority
We are called to stand in this hour
In the Place of His Glory.

Waves of His Glory

Waves and waves of His Glory crashing over me
Waves and waves of His Love washing over me
Waves and waves of His Peace, it is consuming me
Waves and waves of His Fire, it is igniting me
Waves of Revival Fire that are beckoning me
Waves and waves of Healing restoring me.

As I beheld my King, tears filled His eyes
I looked around Heaven there was a hushed sound
For the angels in awe
And His saints on the ground
the joy set before Him, he now beheld.
Tears rolling down the cheeks of the Father
As the sounds of pure worship touched His Heart.

Building a Wall of Praise

We're building a wall of praise
We're building a wall of praise
Building a wall of praise
That the enemy can't take down

Stone by stone, built on one another
Walls of might reaching even higher
We're standing as one loving one another
That His Glory may dwell in this place

May we be one in Jesus
As Jesus was one in the Father
That we may know His Glory
Let Jesus' prayer be fulfilled in us.

The Walls are Tumbling Down

His people cry Glory
His people cry Holy
His people shout Hallelujah
His people declare the Victory

See the walls come tumbling down
With shouts of Victory
See resistance falling down
With our praise unto the King

Lift up your praise
Dance Your Victory Dance!
Giving Glory to the King
Amidst the circumstance!

Dance that He may set them free
They are locked up in their body
Locked up in their minds
Trapped by the enemy.

Dance before the King
The dance of deliverance
A dance of intercession
That He may set them free

Lord, you have broken the fetters
You've snapped the chains around their neck
You have opened their spirit
To receive the Word of Truth that sets them free!

They shall know the Truth
And the Truth shall set them free
They shall hear the Truth
And the Truth shall make them Free.

Victory

Jesus, Almighty are You
Jesus, Faithful and true
You have overcome the world
We have Victory in You.

Jesus, you are coming in Power
Jesus, you are raising us this hour.
To be a light in this dark place
We claim victory in You.

Jesus, Your purposes revealed
Lord, Your will shall be fulfilled
Your light shall overcome
We have victory in You.

For they shall know Your Grace
We shall see Your Glory
As we look upon Your face.

For I Know the Grace

For I know the Grace of the Lord Jesus Christ
For though He was poor, yet for my sake
He became poor, that through his poverty
I am made rich.

I reach up by faith to receive in full
The inheritance that Jesus paid for.
For it's not by my works
But it's by His Grace alone
So I stand on His Word
And claim it by faith.

For I know the Grace of the Lord Jesus Christ
For though He was poor, yet for my sake
He became poor, that through his poverty I am made rich.

Armed

Armed with strength, might and power
Raised in His Glory, this is the hour.

We stand in Jesus, we stand in Victory
We stand in Jesus, for all eternity
We stand in Jesus, we stand in Victory
We stand in Jesus, He's making History.

Jesus is coming!
He's coming to set things straight.
Jesus is coming!
He is standing near the gate!
Jesus is coming!
He's setting the captives free.
Jesus is coming!
The deaf will hear,
The blind will see!

Armed with strength, might and power
Raised in His Glory, this is the hour.

We stand in Jesus, we stand in Victory
We stand in Jesus, for all eternity
We stand in Jesus, we stand in Victory
We stand in Jesus, He's making History.

POETIC PONDERINGS
of the
Heart

When I Get to Heaven

When I get to Heaven is a song that Raelynn Parkin began in 1993 but never finished. When her husband Paul began to write a children's Easter play, this song found its perfected form. This song is about a child who is captive in a wheel chair but dreams of one day walking if not in this earth then with Jesus in Heaven.

They gathered one day in Sunday School
They talked of dreams of who they'd be
One shy little psalmist began to say
This is who I want to be someday.

When I get to Heaven, I want to sing like David
When I get to Heaven, I want my song to touch God's own heart
When I get to heaven, A royal King and Priest I'll be
Oh God please hear my prayer
I want to be like David when I get there.

Then another child spoke
He stuttered and clammered for every word he could
All of Heaven turned their ear
As he spoke his imperfect prayer.

When I get to Heaven, I want to be like Moses
When I get to Heaven, I want to speak and the waters part
When I get to Heaven, Signs and wonders I'll declare
Oh God please hear my prayer
I want to be like Moses when I get there.

179

One child sat straight up
With excitement in his face
As he straightened his legs in his wheelchair
He closed his eyes to imagine he could be
As he spoke these words of faith.

When I get to heaven, I want to walk like Jesus
When I get to Heaven, I want to walk the streets of gold.
When I get to Heaven, I want to walk with my Jesus.
Oh God, please hear my prayer,
I want to be like Jesus when I get there.

When I get to heaven, I want to walk like Jesus
When I get to Heaven,
The lame shall walk and the dumb shall speak,
When I get to Heaven, I want to walk with my Jesus.
Oh God, please hear my prayer,
I want to be like Jesus when I get there.

Rooted and Grounded

Rooted and grounded in His Love
Rooted in the Love of my Father
Established in the Peace of his Rest
A Love that endures forever.
I know the height, the depth, the length, the breadth
For His Love establishes me
Rooted and grounded in the Love of my Father
Immovable for eternity.

Not Him

Not Him is a personal narrative by a worshipper who loved Jesus, watching the Savior as he journeyed to the cross. The death, burial and resurrection are displayed through this entire song. Very powerful and very moving. It was written exactly one year before the Passion of the Christ hit the theaters, and when it was written, Raelynn was writing this song in the theater while waiting for another movie.

The road was paved with good intentions
The crowd was unified that day
The sky grew dark and threatened rain
Some said a storm would come this way.
Then down a winding path, I saw
Two splintered logs that made a cross.
And one man I couldn't even see his eyes
Thru blood, sweat, and tears, he faintly cried.

(I said,) Not Him, I saw him feed five thousand
Not Him, He made blind eyes see,
Not Him, He loved the unlovely
Not Him, He touched my life and I will never be the same.

They lifted Him up for all men to see
The anguish and pain transformed his face.
They mocked Him, and cast lots for His clothes,
They were insane.
The man who gave hope, was dying there alone in utter shame.
I heard Him cry, "Father, forgive them,"
And with His last breath, He hung his head, and died.

(I cried), Not Him, I saw Him walk upon the water.
Not Him, He set a captive man free.
Not Him, He healed the lepers, and raised the dead.
Not Him, He touched my life and I will never be the same.

It's Him, they said they saw Him alive
It's Him, He rose again like He said He would.
It's Him, He paid my price I could not pay.
It's Him, He gave me life, and I will never be the same.

He is Calling You

He is Calling You is a personal invitation from the Lord Jesus Himself welcoming all those who are weary to come to Him. Very moving and anointed in its performance.

He is calling you to come today
Jesus won't ever turn you away
For He laid down His life for you
To give you life anew.

If you feel Him drawing you today
Come to Jesus, don't turn Him away
Surrender your life to the One
Who loves you and makes you complete.

He is calling you to come today
Jesus won't ever turn you away.

Pressed

I am being pressed, shaped, and molded for Your Glory
Pressed, shaped and molded for Your Pleasure
Pressed, shaped and molded
To carry Your Light to the nations.

Yes, I embrace your touch
Though it may bruise me.
I embrace your touch
Though it might hurt me.
I embrace Your Loving touch
As it is shaping me to carry Your Glory.
For you are shaping me to carry Your Glory.

I am being pressed, shaped, and molded for Your Glory
Pressed, shaped and molded for Your Pleasure
Pressed, shaped and molded
To carry Your Light to the nations.

For I shall not be removed.
I shall not be removed
From where you have placed me, Oh Lord.
I am safe in Your Hand.

I am being pressed, shaped, and molded for Your Glory
Pressed, shaped and molded for Your Pleasure
Pressed, shaped and molded to carry Your Light to the
nations.

Ignite Our Hearts

Holy Spirit, like a rushing wind
Like a raging River
Pour through us again.
Your burning Fire, From the Father's Glory
Ignite the Flame within.
Ignite our hearts again.

Give us new revelation of who Jesus is.
Kindle our worship as we glorify His Name.
Give us new revelation of who Jesus is.
Kindle our worship as we glorify His Name.
Jesus.

Holy Spirit, like a rushing wind
Like a raging River
Pour through us again.
Your burning Fire, From the Father's Glory
Ignite the Flame within.
Ignite our hearts again.

Give us Living Water
We are thirsty for His Word.
Strength, to do the Will of the Father in the earth.
Holy Spirit reveal to us the Glory of the Son
Holy Spirit rain down on us the Glory of the Father.
Let the Glory of the Father Kiss the Glory of the Son.
A Kiss for all eternity – One!

Who Will Cry my Tears?

Who will cry my tears for them
That flow from My Heart?
Who will care for my little lost ones,
Enough to count the cost?
For I cry for them, like I cried for you.
Who will go for me, I'm asking you?

Who will go because I asked them to?
Who will go and take my love to them, will you?
For the Heart of My Father
Nothing less will do
Who will love them, as I have loved you?

Who will extend my Hand to them,
To pull them from the mire?
Who will stand in front of them?
For that is My Desire.
For I died for them, like I died for you.
Who will stand for them? I'm calling you.

Who will go because I asked them to?
Who will go and take my love to them, will you?
For the Heart of My Father
Nothing less will do
Who will love them, as I have loved you?

I will go, because You asked me to.
We will go, and take your Love to them for You.

For the Heart of Our King, Nothing less will do.
We will love them, because we love you.

We will love them, Jesus
We will love them
You've entrusted them to us.
We will love them, Jesus
We will love them
You've entrusted them to us.

We will go, because You asked us to.
We will go, and take your Love to them for You.
For the Heart of Our King, Nothing less will do.
We will love them, because we love you.

Man of Honor

This song was birthed two weeks after the September 11, 2001 tragedy in America. A tribute and an Honor to the fallen.

Man of honor, man of strength
Living in the arms of His Savior
Taken by hand, carving the path,
Laying his life down for the nations.

Heart of a servant, love for all.
Crying the tears of His Savior
Dead to this life, but alive in Christ
Living out the gospel before Heaven.

We stand (sing) in honor of this general,
Who is rising to the call of his Father
Counting the cost, trading His Life
To capture the Pearl of Great Price.

Woman of honor, woman of strength
Living in the arms of Her Savior
Taken by hand, carving the path,
Laying her life down for the nations.

We stand (sing) in honor of this general,
Who is rising to the call of her Father
Counting the cost, trading Her Life
To capture the Pearl of Great Price.

Wisdom's House

Don't you listen, she cries out to you.
Come in here, I've prepared you my food.
Oh foolish one, don't walk down the way
To her house, she'll lead you astray.

Her name is your flesh, on your life she will feed.
Don't taste of her food, or more you will need.
Give her an inch, and she'll take you a mile.
With her flattery and deceptive smile.

I exalt Your Name Lord
I stand on Your Word.
I am blessed, not crushed
I shall overcome by the Precious Blood of the Lamb.

Wisdom calls from her house inside
Her table is spread with Heavenly finds
By her Kings rule, and judges prevail
She'll keep your feet on the Path of Life.

I exalt Your Name Lord
I stand on Your Word.
I am blessed, not crushed
I shall overcome by the Precious Blood of the Lamb.
I exalt Your Name Lord
I stand on Your Word.
I am Victory Bound, I am Heaven found
Living in Wisdom's House.

Though the enemy accuses and shames me.
The new man in me shall rise up to see
One hundred fold Victory.

Heart Song

Let us touch the Heart of our Father
Let us touch the Heart of our King
Holy Spirit, stretch forth worship
With our love and our praises we bring.

With our hearts we cry, Abba Father
With our love, we honor our King
With our spirit we long to know your Presence
Spirit flow through our heart song.

Let us come closer to the Throne of our Father
Let us go higher in the Love of our King
Holy Spirit anoint us in worship
With our love and our praises we bring.

Abba Father, we love and adore You
Precious Jesus, we praise your Holy Name
Holy Spirit we bless your Awesome Presence
With one voice we worship our God
Anoint us as we worship our God!

Make Room for Him

A young man in his twenties
He was pledged to marry
A young girl of his dreams
Or so it would seem
She told him of a child to come
His heart said where did this come from?
Was this not the girl of my dreams?
Oh God, how could this be?
And He said…

My son, she is the one
I've chosen to carry my only begotten Son
The Promised Deliverer who will set you free
Make room for Him in your heart
This day I have set you apart.

So he took Mary as his wife
He shared her trials, he shared her life.
They set out on a journey to the place of his birth
To bring forth this Child of Great Worth.
The time had come to deliver the Promise
He'd waited so long, His time was now upon us.
As light came forth to a dark and thirsty world
That was unprepared to take Him in.

My son, you are the ones
I've chosen to deliver my only begotten Son
The Promised Redeemer who'll set my people free

Though none made room for Him
He has come to bring life to men.

He came to seek and save that which was lost.
To bring a dying world back to His Father's Arms.

My sons, my daughters you are the ones
I've chosen to proclaim my only begotten Son
The Promised Redeemer who will set them free
Make room for Him in Your Heart
For this day I have set you apart
Make room for Jesus in Your Heart.

Who will That be?

Who can I find that looks like me?
Who will hold and embrace my baby boy?
Who will stand guard and protect my Son?
Who can I find that my Son will look up to,
That I can love through,
That He can look through his eyes and find Me?
Who will that be?

Who can I find that is set apart?
Who can I find who carries My Heart?
Who will love one that's not his own?
Who will teach Him my ways,
Who will show Him such grace,
Who can I trust to be a father to Him
Who looks like me?

My eyes are searching through generations
Who will lay down his life before Him
Who will stand before and deliver My Son
To the cross that He may save the world?
Who will that be?
Who can I find that looks like me?
Who can I trust with my baby boy?
Who will that be?

Joy

Cold and still in a dark lonely place
The Hope of the World waits for me
Light from the Heavens, streams from above
As the Light of the World comes for me.

Joy, Joy, the whole world sings
Joy for the Baby is born.
Joy, Joy, rejoice all His People
Joy for the Lord has come.

The Glory of Heaven reveals His Name
For a dying world
The gift of Salvation He brings.

Joy, Joy, the whole world sings
Joy for the Baby is born.
Joy, Joy, rejoice all His People
Joy for the Lord has come.

For Joy to the world, the Lord has come
With Peace and Joy, His Gift of Salvation
Wrapped in His Perfect Love.

Joy, Joy, the whole world sings
Joy for the Baby is born.
Joy, Joy, rejoice all His People
Joy for the Lord has come.

BIBLICAL POETIC
INSIGHTS
Song of
Songs

Here are the most beautiful Bride Psalms ever recorded. Be swept away by the poetry of the romance in scripture...

1 Solomon's Song of Songs.

She

² Let him kiss me with the kisses of his mouth—
  for your love is more delightful than wine.
³ Pleasing is the fragrance of your perfumes;
  your name is like perfume poured out.
  No wonder the young women love you!
⁴ Take me away with you—let us hurry!
  Let the king bring me into his chambers.

Friends

We rejoice and delight in you;
  we will praise your love more than wine.

She

How right they are to adore you!
⁵ Dark am I, yet lovely,
  daughters of Jerusalem,
dark like the tents of Kedar,
  like the tent curtains of Solomon.
⁶ Do not stare at me because I am dark,
  because I am darkened by the sun.
My mother's sons were angry with me
  and made me take care of the vineyards;
  my own vineyard I had to neglect.

⁷ Tell me, you whom I love,
   where you graze your flock
   and where you rest your sheep at midday.
Why should I be like a veiled woman
   beside the flocks of your friends?

Friends

⁸ If you do not know, most beautiful of women,
   follow the tracks of the sheep
and graze your young goats
   by the tents of the shepherds.

He

⁹ I liken you, my darling, to a mare
   among Pharaoh's chariot horses.
¹⁰ Your cheeks are beautiful with earrings,
   your neck with strings of jewels.
¹¹ We will make you earrings of gold,
   studded with silver.

She

¹² While the king was at his table,
   my perfume spread its fragrance.
¹³ My beloved is to me a sachet of myrrh
   resting between my breasts.
¹⁴ My beloved is to me a cluster of henna blossoms
   from the vineyards of En Gedi.

He

¹⁵ How beautiful you are, my darling!
   Oh, how beautiful!
   Your eyes are doves.

She

¹⁶ How handsome you are, my beloved!
   Oh, how charming!
   And our bed is verdant.

He

¹⁷ The beams of our house are cedars;
   our rafters are firs.

She

2 I am a rose of Sharon,
   a lily of the valleys.

He

² Like a lily among thorns
   is my darling among the young women.

She

³ Like an apple tree among the trees of the forest
   is my beloved among the young men.
I delight to sit in his shade,
   and his fruit is sweet to my taste.
⁴ Let him lead me to the banquet hall,
   and let his banner over me be love.

⁵ Strengthen me with raisins,
    refresh me with apples,
    for I am faint with love.
⁶ His left arm is under my head,
    and his right arm embraces me.
⁷ Daughters of Jerusalem, I charge you
    by the gazelles and by the does of the field:
Do not arouse or awaken love
    until it so desires.
⁸ Listen! My beloved!
    Look! Here he comes,
leaping across the mountains,
    bounding over the hills.
⁹ My beloved is like a gazelle or a young stag.
    Look! There he stands behind our wall,
gazing through the windows,
    peering through the lattice.
¹⁰ My beloved spoke and said to me,
    "Arise, my darling,
    my beautiful one, come with me.
¹¹ See! The winter is past;
    the rains are over and gone.
¹² Flowers appear on the earth;
    the season of singing has come,
the cooing of doves
    is heard in our land.
¹³ The fig tree forms its early fruit;
    the blossoming vines spread their fragrance.

Arise, come, my darling;
   my beautiful one, come with me."
He

¹⁴ My dove in the clefts of the rock,
   in the hiding places on the mountainside,
show me your face,
   let me hear your voice;
for your voice is sweet,
   and your face is lovely.
¹⁵ Catch for us the foxes,
   the little foxes
that ruin the vineyards,
   our vineyards that are in bloom.

She

¹⁶ My beloved is mine and I am his;
   he browses among the lilies.
¹⁷ Until the day breaks
   and the shadows flee,
turn, my beloved,
   and be like a gazelle
or like a young stag
   on the rugged hills.

3 All night long on my bed
   I looked for the one my heart loves;
   I looked for him but did not find him.
² I will get up now and go about the city,
   through its streets and squares;

I will search for the one my heart loves.
So I looked for him but did not find him.
³ The watchmen found me
as they made their rounds in the city.
"Have you seen the one my heart loves?"
⁴ Scarcely had I passed them
when I found the one my heart loves.
I held him and would not let him go
till I had brought him to my mother's house,
to the room of the one who conceived me.
⁵ Daughters of Jerusalem, I charge you
by the gazelles and by the does of the field:
Do not arouse or awaken love
until it so desires.
⁶ Who is this coming up from the wilderness
like a column of smoke,
perfumed with myrrh and incense
made from all the spices of the merchant?
⁷ Look! It is Solomon's carriage,
escorted by sixty warriors,
the noblest of Israel,
⁸ all of them wearing the sword,
all experienced in battle,
each with his sword at his side,
prepared for the terrors of the night.
⁹ King Solomon made for himself the carriage;
he made it of wood from Lebanon.
¹⁰ Its posts he made of silver,
its base of gold.

Its seat was upholstered with purple,
   its interior inlaid with love.
Daughters of Jerusalem, [11] come out,
   and look, you daughters of Zion.
Look on King Solomon wearing a crown,
   the crown with which his mother crowned him
on the day of his wedding,
   the day his heart rejoiced.

He

4 How beautiful you are, my darling!
   Oh, how beautiful!
   Your eyes behind your veil are doves.
Your hair is like a flock of goats
   descending from the hills of Gilead.
[2] Your teeth are like a flock of sheep just shorn,
   coming up from the washing.
Each has its twin;
   not one of them is alone.
[3] Your lips are like a scarlet ribbon;
   your mouth is lovely.
Your temples behind your veil
   are like the halves of a pomegranate.
[4] Your neck is like the tower of David,
   built with courses of stone;
on it hang a thousand shields,
   all of them shields of warriors.
[5] Your breasts are like two fawns,

like twin fawns of a gazelle
  that browse among the lilies.
⁶ Until the day breaks
  and the shadows flee,
I will go to the mountain of myrrh
  and to the hill of incense.
⁷ You are altogether beautiful, my darling;
  there is no flaw in you.
⁸ Come with me from Lebanon, my bride,
  come with me from Lebanon.
Descend from the crest of Amana,
  from the top of Senir, the summit of Hermon,
from the lions' dens
  and the mountain haunts of leopards.
⁹ You have stolen my heart, my sister, my bride;
  you have stolen my heart
with one glance of your eyes,
  with one jewel of your necklace.
¹⁰ How delightful is your love, my sister, my bride!
  How much more pleasing is your love than wine,
and the fragrance of your perfume
  more than any spice!
¹¹ Your lips drop sweetness as the honeycomb, my bride;
  milk and honey are under your tongue.
The fragrance of your garments
  is like the fragrance of Lebanon.
¹² You are a garden locked up, my sister, my bride;
  you are a spring enclosed, a sealed fountain.
¹³ Your plants are an orchard of pomegranates

with choice fruits,
    with henna and nard,
14 nard and saffron,
    calamus and cinnamon,
    with every kind of incense tree,
    with myrrh and aloes
    and all the finest spices.
15 You are a garden fountain,
    a well of flowing water
    streaming down from Lebanon.

She

16 Awake, north wind,
    and come, south wind!
Blow on my garden,
    that its fragrance may spread everywhere.
Let my beloved come into his garden
    and taste its choice fruits.

He

5 I have come into my garden, my sister, my bride;
    I have gathered my myrrh with my spice.
I have eaten my honeycomb and my honey;
    I have drunk my wine and my milk.

Friends

Eat, friends, and drink;
    drink your fill of love.

She

²I slept but my heart was awake.
 Listen! My beloved is knocking:
"Open to me, my sister, my darling,
 my dove, my flawless one.
My head is drenched with dew,
 my hair with the dampness of the night."
³I have taken off my robe—
 must I put it on again?
I have washed my feet—
 must I soil them again?
⁴My beloved thrust his hand through the latch-opening;
 my heart began to pound for him.
⁵I arose to open for my beloved,
 and my hands dripped with myrrh,
my fingers with flowing myrrh,
 on the handles of the bolt.
⁶I opened for my beloved,
 but my beloved had left; he was gone.
 My heart sank at his departure.
I looked for him but did not find him.
 I called him but he did not answer.
⁷The watchmen found me
 as they made their rounds in the city.
They beat me, they bruised me;
 they took away my cloak,
 those watchmen of the walls!
⁸Daughters of Jerusalem, I charge you—

if you find my beloved,
what will you tell him?
  Tell him I am faint with love.

Friends

⁹ How is your beloved better than others,
  most beautiful of women?
How is your beloved better than others,
  that you so charge us?

She

¹⁰ My beloved is radiant and ruddy,
  outstanding among ten thousand.
¹¹ His head is purest gold;
  his hair is wavy
  and black as a raven.
¹² His eyes are like doves
  by the water streams,
washed in milk,
  mounted like jewels.
¹³ His cheeks are like beds of spice
  yielding perfume.
His lips are like lilies
  dripping with myrrh.
¹⁴ His arms are rods of gold
  set with topaz.
His body is like polished ivory
  decorated with lapis lazuli.
¹⁵ His legs are pillars of marble

set on bases of pure gold.
His appearance is like Lebanon,
  choice as its cedars.
¹⁶ His mouth is sweetness itself;
  he is altogether lovely.
This is my beloved, this is my friend,
  daughters of Jerusalem.

Friends

6 Where has your beloved gone,
  most beautiful of women?
Which way did your beloved turn,
  that we may look for him with you?

She

² My beloved has gone down to his garden,
  to the beds of spices,
to browse in the gardens
  and to gather lilies.
³ I am my beloved's and my beloved is mine;
  he browses among the lilies.

He

⁴ You are as beautiful as Tirzah, my darling,
  as lovely as Jerusalem,
  as majestic as troops with banners.
⁵ Turn your eyes from me;
  they overwhelm me.
Your hair is like a flock of goats

descending from Gilead.

⁶ Your teeth are like a flock of sheep
   coming up from the washing.
Each has its twin,
   not one of them is missing.
⁷ Your temples behind your veil
   are like the halves of a pomegranate.
⁸ Sixty queens there may be,
   and eighty concubines,
   and virgins beyond number;
⁹ but my dove, my perfect one, is unique,
   the only daughter of her mother,
   the favorite of the one who bore her.
The young women saw her and called her blessed;
   the queens and concubines praised her.

Friends

¹⁰ Who is this that appears like the dawn,
   fair as the moon, bright as the sun,
   majestic as the stars in procession?

He

¹¹ I went down to the grove of nut trees
   to look at the new growth in the valley,
to see if the vines had budded
   or the pomegranates were in bloom.
¹² Before I realized it,
   my desire set me among the royal chariots of my people.

Friends

¹³ Come back, come back, O Shulammite;
   come back, come back, that we may gaze on you!
He

Why would you gaze on the Shulammite
   as on the dance of Mahanaim?

7 How beautiful your sandaled feet,
   O prince's daughter!
Your graceful legs are like jewels,
   the work of an artist's hands.
² Your navel is a rounded goblet
   that never lacks blended wine.
Your waist is a mound of wheat
   encircled by lilies.
³ Your breasts are like two fawns,
   like twin fawns of a gazelle.
⁴ Your neck is like an ivory tower.
Your eyes are the pools of Heshbon
   by the gate of Bath Rabbim.
Your nose is like the tower of Lebanon
   looking toward Damascus.
⁵ Your head crowns you like Mount Carmel.
   Your hair is like royal tapestry;
   the king is held captive by its tresses.
⁶ How beautiful you are and how pleasing,
   my love, with your delights!
⁷ Your stature is like that of the palm,

and your breasts like clusters of fruit.
⁸ I said, "I will climb the palm tree;
   I will take hold of its fruit."
May your breasts be like clusters of grapes on the vine,
   the fragrance of your breath like apples,
⁹   and your mouth like the best wine.

She

May the wine go straight to my beloved,
   flowing gently over lips and teeth.
¹⁰ I belong to my beloved,
   and his desire is for me.
¹¹ Come, my beloved, let us go to the countryside,
   let us spend the night in the villages.
¹² Let us go early to the vineyards
   to see if the vines have budded,
if their blossoms have opened,
   and if the pomegranates are in bloom—
   there I will give you my love.
¹³ The mandrakes send out their fragrance,
   and at our door is every delicacy,
both new and old,
   that I have stored up for you, my beloved.

8 If only you were to me like a brother,
   who was nursed at my mother's breasts!
Then, if I found you outside,
   I would kiss you,
   and no one would despise me.

²I would lead you
   and bring you to my mother's house—
   she who has taught me.
I would give you spiced wine to drink,
   the nectar of my pomegranates.
³His left arm is under my head
   and his right arm embraces me.
⁴Daughters of Jerusalem, I charge you:
   Do not arouse or awaken love
   until it so desires.

Friends

⁵Who is this coming up from the wilderness
   leaning on her beloved?

She

Under the apple tree I roused you;
   there your mother conceived you,
   there she who was in labor gave you birth.
⁶Place me like a seal over your heart,
   like a seal on your arm;
for love is as strong as death,
   its jealousy unyielding as the grave.
It burns like blazing fire,
   like a mighty flame.
⁷Many waters cannot quench love;
   rivers cannot sweep it away.
If one were to give

all the wealth of one's house for love,
  it would be utterly scorned.

Friends

[8] We have a little sister,
  and her breasts are not yet grown.
What shall we do for our sister
  on the day she is spoken for?
[9] If she is a wall,
  we will build towers of silver on her.
If she is a door,
  we will enclose her with panels of cedar.

She

[10] I am a wall,
  and my breasts are like towers.
Thus I have become in his eyes
  like one bringing contentment.
[11] Solomon had a vineyard in Baal Hamon;
  he let out his vineyard to tenants.
Each was to bring for its fruit
  a thousand shekels of silver.
[12] But my own vineyard is mine to give;
  the thousand shekels are for you, Solomon,
  and two hundred are for those who tend its fruit.

He

[13] You who dwell in the gardens
  with friends in attendance,
  let me hear your voice!

She

[14] Come away, my beloved,
  and be like a gazelle
or like a young stag
  on the spice-laden mountains.

Other Resources by Bride Song Ministries

Books and Teaching Resources

Unlocking Worship Entering His Presence $15.95

This book explores worship ministry according to the Word of God, exposes the strategies of the enemy that hinder the Glory, establishes precepts of the worshiping priesthood and ultimately declares what must be present to see the glory of God return back to the Church, especially the American Church.

The Heavenly Worship Room $15.95

The Revelation unfolded in the context of Today's Prophetic Hour for the Church and the Jewish Nation.

Unlocking Worship Workbook $10.00

This workbook corresponds to the first edition of *Lessons from One Worship Leader to Another*, which is updated in *Unlocking Worship Entering His Presence*. This workbook accompanies the book *Unlocking Worship Entering His Presence* and the *Unlocking Teaching Series* to enforce the principles of worship ministry and the Glory for the worshipper, the worship leader or pastor. It is broken up into 8 weeks with daily work for the hungry student/worshipper.

Unlocking Worship Teaching CD Series
8 sessions $40.00

This teaching series builds upon the original principles of the book, *Lessons from One Worship Leader to Another*, (now in its second edition, the updated version *Unlocking Worship Entering His Presence*) with fresh revelation, anointing and application above and beyond what is contained in the book.

Music CDs

The Lord's Bridal Company Vol. 1 CD $10.00

A Live Worship Night Experience soaking in an atmosphere of Heaven.

The Lord's Bridal Company Vol. 2 $15.00

A live recording featuring 11 musicians prophesying the intimate songs from *Out of the Secret Place* and the Bride Songs Studio projects.

Out of the Secret Place $15.00

Throne Room Worship from the Secret Place.

Bride Songs A Lady and Her King $15.00

A treasury of Songs of romance from the Bride to the King.

Arise My Church Arise Live CD $15.00

The live recording from the *Arise My Church Arise Summer Houston Tour* featuring 11 prophetic artists.

To order these resources, go to
www.bridesongministries.org
Or www.raelynnparkin.com

Or email your request to
bridesong.raelynn@gmail.com
Or via mail, write your check to Bride Song Ministries, to include $5 shipping/handling, and mail to:
Bride Song Ministries
18311 Trace Forest Drive
Spring, Texas 77379

Also visit our YouTube Worship Channel BridesongMinistries1 or follow us on Facebook Bride Song Ministries Page.

www.ingramcontent.com/pod-product-compliance
Lightning Source LLC
Chambersburg PA
CBHW021827090426
42811CB00032B/2056/J